HARMONY

IN

MARRIAGE

- Dada Bhagwan

A Translation of Gujarati Abridged Version

Editor : Dr. Niruben Amin

Publisher : **Mr. Ajit C. Patel**
Dada Bhagwan Aradhana Trust
Dada Darshan, 5, Mamta Park Soc,
B/h. Navgujrat College, Usmanpura,
Ahmedabad-380014,
Gujarat, India.
Tel. : +91 79 3983 0100

First Edition : 3000 copies, February 2001
Second Edition : 2000 copies, October 2004
Third Edition : 2000 copies, January 2008
Fourth Edition : 3000 copies, January 2014

Price   : Ultimate Humility (leads to Universal oneness)
and Awareness of "I Don't Know Anything"

Rs. 25.00

Printer   : Amba Offset
Basement, Parshwanath Chambers,
Nr. RBI, Usmanpura,
Ahmedabad-380014, Gujarat, India.
Tel. : +91 79 27542964

Trimantra

The Three Mantras that Destroy All Obstacles in Life

Namo Vitaragaya
I bow to the One who is absolutely free from all attachment and abhorrence

Namo Arihantanam
I bow to the living One who has annihilated all internal enemies of anger, pride, deceit and greed

Namo Siddhanam
I bow to the Ones who have attained the state of total and final liberation

Namo Aayariyanam
I bow to the Self-realized masters who impart knowledge of liberation to others

Namo Uvazzayanam
I bow to those who have received the Knowledge of the Self and are helping others attain the same

Namo Loye Savva Sahunam
I bow to all saints everywhere who have received the Knowledge of the Self

Eso Pancha Namukkaro
These five salutations

Savva Pavappanasano
Destroy all demerit karma

Mangalanam cha Savvesim
Of all that is auspicious

Padhamam Havai Mangalam
This is the highest

Om Namo Bhagavate Vasudevaya
I bow to all who have attained the absolute Self in human form

Om Namah Shivaya
I bow to all human beings who have become instruments for salvation of the world

Jai Sat Chit Anand
Awareness of the Eternal is Bliss

Note About This Translation

Gnani Purush Ambalal M. Patel, popularly known as Dadashri or Dada or Dadaji, used to say that it is not possible to exactly translate his satsang on the Science of Self-Realization and the art of worldly interaction, into English. Some of the depth and intent of meaning to be conveyed to the seeker, would be lost. He stressed the importance of learning Gujarati to precisely understand all his teachings.

Dadashri did however grant his blessings to convey his original words to the world through translations in English and other languages. It was his deepest desire and fervor that the suffering human beings of the world attain the living freedom of the wonderful Akram Vignan that expressed within him. He further stated that a day would come when the world would be in awe of the phenomenal powers of this science.

This is an humble attempt to present to the world the essence of the teachings of Dadashri, the Gnani Purush. A lot of care has been taken to preserve the tone and message of his words. This is not a literal translation of his words. Many individuals have worked diligently for this product and we remain deeply thankful to them all.

This is an elementary introduction to the vast new treasure of his teachings. Please note that any errors committed in the translation are entirely those of the translators and for those we request your pardon.

❖❖❖❖❖

4

Introduction to The 'Gnani Purush'

On a June evening in 1958 at around six o'clock, Ambalal Muljibhai Patel, a family man, a contractor by profession, was sitting on a bench on the busy platform number 3 of Surat's train station. Surat is a city in south Gujarat, a western state in India. What happened within the next forty-eight minutes was phenomenal. Spontaneous Self-realization occurred within Ambalal M. Patel. During this event his ego completely melted and from that moment onwards he became completely detached from all Ambalal's thoughts, speech and acts. He became the Lord's living instrument for the salvation of mankind, through the path of knowledge. He called this Lord, Dada Bhagwan. To everyone he met, he would say, "This Lord, Dada Bhagwan is fully manifest within me. He also resides within all living beings. The difference is that within me He is completely expressed and in you, he is yet to manifest."

Who are we? What is God? Who runs this world? What is karma? What is liberation? Etc. All the world's spiritual questions were answered during this event. Thus nature offered absolute vision to the world through the medium of Shree Ambalal Muljibhai Patel.

Ambalal was born in Tarsali, a suburb of the city of Baroda and raised in Bhadran, Gujarat. His wife's name was Hiraba. Although he was a contractor by profession, his life at home and his interaction with everyone around him was exemplary even prior to his Self-realization. After becoming Self-realized and attaining the state of a Gnani, (The Awakened One), his body became a 'public charitable trust.'

Throughout his whole life he lived by the principle that there should not be any commerce in religion, and in all commerce there must be religion. He also never took money from anyone for his own use. He used the profits from his business to take his devotees for pilgrimages to various parts of India.

His words became the foundation for the new, direct and step-less path to Self-realization called Akram Vignan. Through his divine original scientific experiment (The Gnan Vidhi), he imparted this knowledge to others within two hours. Thousands have received his grace through this process and thousands continue to do so even now. 'Akram' means without steps; an elevator path or a short cut, whereas 'Kram' means an orderly step-by-step spiritual path. Akram is now recognized as a direct shortcut to the bliss of the Self.

Who is Dada Bhagwan ?

When he explained to others who 'Dada Bhagwan' is, he would say:

"What you see here is not 'Dada Bhagwan.' What you see is 'A.M.Patel.' I am a Gnani Purush and He that is manifest within me, is 'Dada Bhagwan'. He is the Lord within. He is within you and everyone else. He has not yet manifest within you, whereas within me he is fully manifest. I myself am not a Bhagwan. I too bow down to Dada Bhagwan within me."

Current link for attaining the knowledge of Self-Realization (Atmagnan)

"I am personally going to impart siddhis (special spiritual powers) to a few people. After I leave, will there not be a need for them? People of future generations will need this path, won't they?"

~ **Dadashri**

Param Pujya Dadashri used to go from town to town and country-to-country to give satsang and impart the knowledge of the Self as well as knowledge of harmonious worldly interaction to all who came to see him. In his final days in late 1987, he graced Dr. Niruben Amin with the siddhis to continue his Work.

After Param Pujya Dadashri left his mortal body on January 2, 1988, Dr. Niruben continued his Work, traveling within India to cities and villages; and going abroad visiting all continents of the world. She was Dadashri's representative of Akram Vignan, until March 19, 2006, when she left her mortal body entrusting all further care of the Work to Shri Deepakbhai Desai. She was instrumental in expanding the key role of Akram Vignan as the simple and direct path to Self-realization for modern times. Hundreds of thousands of spiritual seekers had taken advantage of this opportunity and are established in the experience of pure Soul while carrying out their worldly duties. They experience freedom, here and now while living their daily life.

Shri Deepakbhai Desai had been given the siddhi to conduct satsang of Akram Vignan by Gnani Purush Dadashri in presence of Pujya Niruben Amin. Between 1988 and 2006, he has given satsang nationally and internationally as directed by Dadashri under the guidance of Dr. Niruben Amin. Now these satsangs and Gnan Vidhis of Akram Vignan continue in full force through the medium of Atmagnani Shri Deepakbhai Desai.

Powerful words in scriptures help the seeker in increasing their desire for liberation and thus they represent the path. The knowledge of the Self is the final goal of all seekers. Without the knowledge of the Self there is no liberation. This knowledge does not exist in books. It exists in the heart of a Gnani. Hence, the knowledge of the Self can only be acquired by meeting a Gnani. Through the scientific approach of the Akram Vignan, even today one can attain Atmagnan, by meeting a living Atmagnani. Only a lit candle can light another candle!

❖❖❖❖❖

EDITORIAL

Men and women have been around forever. They meet each other, get married, and leave each other, life after life, resulting in complex, worldly interactions between the two. In the previous time cycles of *Satyug, Dwapar,* and *Tretayug,* problems between men and women were nominal due to simplicity of their innate characteristics, which enabled them to adjust easily with one another. In this current time cycle of *Kaliyug,* the nature is such that the personalities of men and women lead to altercations. Married couples constantly find themselves at odds with each other and consequently they find no harmony in their life together. How can a married couple find harmony and freedom amongst the constant stress and tension, in this current time cycle? Are there any scriptures or books they can rely on? What are they to do? For these couples, solutions to their everyday problems can be found in the *satsangs* of the *Gnani Purush,* Dadashri, who spoke in a simple and direct language. Dadashri himself was married and had encountered and experienced the problems of married life, but he was also enlightened to the true nature of the world and the Self (the Soul). Dadashri has answered all kinds of questions regarding the interactions between a husband and a wife. This book is a compilation of thousands of questions proposed to the *Gnani Purush,* over a period of thirty years following his spontaneous Self-realization. Couples came to him seeking the ultimate solutions to their turbulent and troubled, married lives.

For the reader who pays attention to the *satsang* that follows in these pages, the grace of the *Gnani* will indeed be imparted upon him or her. They will find peace within themselves and harmony in their home. The solutions given by the *Gnani* will bring closure to the very intricate, complex problems of married life. These answers of the *Gnani,* directly reach the hearts of the readers, blessing them with the divine

8

vision to look upon their life partners as celestial beings.

Many scriptures contain profound knowledge about the reality of this universe. However, this knowledge can only be obtained through words. The scriptures cannot take you beyond this point. Only someone who has lived through a similar experience and has expert knowledge on how to do so can mend shattered lives. *Pujya* Dadashri was a *Gnani* who had absolute knowledge of the Soul, but he was also a married man. His interactions with his wife were nothing short of ideal. Dada's *satsangs,* which are based on his own experiences, provide a simple and direct solution to all of life's problems. His words are the foundation for an ideal life between a husband and a wife. In this current time cycle, this *Akram Vignani* (Scientist of the Step-less Path to Liberation) is a unique and extraordinary gift to the world. The power of his words and his precise answers to the daily problems and interactions that we experience and engage in, are especially phenomenal. No one else has given answers with such clarity and effect.

Several married couples approached Dadashri with the difficulties that they were experiencing in their marriages; some discussions took place in privacy, while others took place out in the open. Dadshri's answers were focused on the questioner's specific situation. Dada has become instrumental in the path of salvation for all couples that long to live in harmony and find real love and meaning in their lives. At times it appeared that Dada scolded only the husbands or that he picked sides, however what he said to them, he said in words that had the power to forever clear all puzzles and confusion for them. The reader is requested to read the entire book in the correct context and not misuse the final words of the *Gnani.* The aim is to find one's own errors and correct them for the ultimate goal of bliss and harmony.

- **Dr. Niruben Amin**

9

Index

Harmony In Marriage

(Ideal interactions between husband and wife, according to *Param Pujya Dada Bhagwan*)

[1] ONE FAMILY

When does one enjoy life? When the whole day passes without any stress or worries. How can one enjoy life when there are conflicts at home? Conflicts are unacceptable, especially at home. Conflicts may arise with neighbors and others, but why at home? At home one should live life as a family. What is family life? In family life, love should prevail and be present at all times. Where is the family life nowadays? The husband starts complaining about a meal that is not to his liking. Underdeveloped people! Developed people would set aside what they do not like, and eat the rest. Can this not be done? That is a family life. Go quarrel outside. What does "my family" mean? It should mean, "We do not have any conflicts." You should adjust. You should know how to adjust within your family. Adjust everywhere.

Do you have the knowledge of what a functional family is? Although we Indians live as a family, we lack the knowledge of how to live as 'an ideal family'. In foreign countries, people do not understand the concept of 'ideal family'. In the Western culture, when James turns twenty, his parents, William and Mary will tell him, "You must now be independent so that we can live our own lives!" They have not grasped the concept of how to function as a family. If Mary does not get along with William, she will consider a divorce right away. In India, divorce is not an option. We stay together, quarrel, and then sleep in the same room. This is not what life is all about. This is not called 'family life'.

In India, people have their own family doctor. How can you have a family doctor, when you do not even have a family? The family doctor is treated as part of the family, while the wife is treated like an outsider. When the family doctor comes, they do not quarrel with him, even if he leaves behind a big bill. Instead they'll say, "This is our family doctor!" People think they have a status in society by having their own family doctor!

Should you quarrel with a member of the family if he accidentally hurt you? No. You should live like a family; you should not just *pretend* to do so. People put up a facade about being a family. It should not be that way. There should be unity within a family. If your wife gets upset with you, wait awhile and then say to her, "No matter what you say to me and no matter how upset you get with me, I miss you when you are not around!" Tell your wife that you don't like being separated from her. Just go ahead and say this *'Guru Mantra'* (words that give results). You never express your love and appreciation to your wife, do you? What is the problem in doing so? Just tell her you do not like being away from her. You should keep most of your love to yourself, but do share and express some of it.

[2] QUARRELS AT HOME

Dadashri : Do you ever have *kalesh* (quarrels) at home? What do you think about conflicts in the home? Do you like it?

Questioner : The world does not function without quarrels.

Dadashri : Then God will not stay wherever there are quarrels.

Questioner : But there should at least be *some* quarrelling!

Dadashri : No, there should not be *any* quarrelling. Why should there be any quarrelling? What is the reason for quarrelling? Are you comfortable with quarrelling? How many months can you live with conflicts?

Questioner : Not a single moment.

Dadashri : Not even for a month? You get good meals to eat, you wear beautiful jewellery, and yet you quarrel. You quarrel because you do not know how to live life; you do not know the art of living. This is what causes quarrels. All people care about is the art of making money. You do not think about how to live life because your thoughts are preoccupied with making money. Shouldn't you think about this?

Questioner : We should think about it, but everyone has a different approach.

Dadashri : No, everyone's ways are not different, they are all the same. "Dollars! Money! Where can I make money?" When one makes money, he goes to a store to buy something for the house and then brings it home and stares at it. Then when it becomes old, he has to go and buy something else. All day long, he is caught up in this kind of a rut; he is unhappy and stressed. How can one live this kind of a life? Does this suit a human being? There should not be any quarrels (*kalesh*).

Questioner : What are you referring to when you say *'kalesh'*?

Dadashri : When you quarrel and clash with your family members, with outsiders, with your wife, all that quarrelling is referred to as *'kalesh'*. If couples get into an argument and as a result, they avoid each other for a while, then this event is called *'kalesh'*. There is no problem if they get together right away after two to three hours of bickering, but if they argue and stay apart, that is called *'kalesh'*. If they stay apart for twelve hours, then the whole night is spent in *'kalesh'*.

Questioner : Is this tendency towards obstinacy in discord (*kankas*) more prevalent in men or women?

Dadashri : Women have more of this tendency.

Questioner : What is the reason for that?

Dadashri : There are two types of clashes, minor and major. Men tend to get into minor clashes, which do not last. Men tend to forgive and forget easily. These are minor clashes. Women on the other hand, tend to engage in major clashes. They do not recover from clashes quite as easily. Instead, they tend to remember it for a prolonged period of time. It is very difficult for women to let go. Due to their nature, women at times are guilty of turning minor issues into major issues. For example, after a minor disagreement, the husband walks about as if nothing has happened, while the wife walks around sulking.

Questioner : So what should we do to avoid major clashes?

Dadashri : If you do not ignite a small fire she will not kindle it. The fault is yours for igniting the fire in the first place. For example, when you tell her that her food tastes awful and you go around with a frown on your face, you ignite a fire. All these trivial things give rise to minor disputes, which she then coverts into major ones.

Questioner : The important thing is that there should be peace at home.

Dadashri : But how can peace prevail? For peace, you have to understand *dharma* (religion, one's duties, moral code of conduct). You should tell everyone at home, "We are not each other's enemies; nobody has any quarrels with anyone. There is no need to have differences of opinion. Let us share with each other what we have and let us be happy." That is how you should think and do everything. You should never quarrel with people at home. How can you quarrel with people you have to share the same home with? Nobody has ever been happy by making others miserable and we want to be happy by giving happiness. We can only be happy if we make others happy at home. You will be served a good cup of tea with a smile, if you avoid conflicts with this understanding. Otherwise, they will ruin your tea before they serve it to you.

Look how many worries and inner differences there are! A person continues to harbour differences of opinion, yet he thinks he practices religion. Ask him if the quarrelling has ceased in his home. Has it even decreased? Have his worries become less? Does he have at least some peace? To that he will say, "No, but at least I practice religion." You fool! What religion do you have? Being religious means, you are at peace within and regardless of your situation in life you do not have any stress, whether it be internal or external. To revert to your Real nature (the Soul), is the final definition of religion.

If your wife drops a stack of china dishes and glassware, would you be affected by it?

If you are affected or you feel hurt, you cannot refrain from saying something; you cannot prevent turning on your 'radio'. The moment you get hurt, your radio will come on, which in turn will hurt her. Then she will point out, "You act as if you never break anything." It is important to understand that glassware can easily slip and break. If you were to tell her to break the dishes, would she do so? Who or what breaks them? There is no person in this world with an independent strength or power to break even a single dish. All these events that take place are accounts that are being settled, and therefore all you have to do is ask her whether or not she was hurt.

If you both fight over a couch, then throw that couch away. That couch is worth only a few hundred dollars. Is it worth fighting over? It will only sow seeds of hatred. Just get rid of it. Anything that causes conflicts in the home should be thrown away.

The more you understand, the greater your faith. With faith you will acquire results. Without faith, nothing will help you. If you do things with understanding, your life will be happy and it will make her life happy too. Does your wife not cook you wonderful meals?

Questioner : Yes, she does.

Dadashri : What more do you need then? Shouldn't you be obligated to her since she is your partner? What is her obligation in this? You bring home the money and she cooks and cleans. This is the way a partnership works. The children are the products of your partnership. They are not solely hers, are they? Just because *she* was the one who went through pregnancy does not mean that they belong only to *her.* Your children belong to the both of you. Do they belong to you both or her alone?

Questioner : Both of us.

Dadashri : Yes. Would men be willing to go through pregnancy? Therefore, this world is worth understanding. It needs to be understood from many different perspectives. Only a *Gnani Purush* can make you understand the world as it is. He enables you to understand what is good for you and what is bad for you. Then there will be an end to the conflicts at home.

Lord Krishna has said there are two kinds of intellect, one is helpful and the other is harmful. The harmful intellect brings forth only pain and misery while the helpful intellect brings forth happiness and seeks out happiness amidst pain and suffering. But what do people do instead? They put grit in their basmati rice and then they eat it! Here in America you get such good food, pure *ghee* and pure yogurt. Life is easy, but people do not know how to live, and that is why they suffer.

We should be thinking about what is beneficial to us. Which of the following is more beneficial, recalling the happiness you experienced on your wedding day or remembering the sorrow of becoming a widower?

The thought of becoming a widower came to me during our marriage ceremony. On my wedding day I was wearing a very stylish and elaborate turban, a kind that royalty would wear at weddings. Dressed in this manner even as a fifteen-year-old groom, I looked very handsome. My attire was bedecked and impressive. Later, as the wedding ceremony was in progress, the turban on my head shifted, obstructing my view. It occurred to me then, that it was fair and well that we were getting married, but one day one of us would have to become a widow.

Questioner : You had such thoughts at that young an age?

Dadashri : Yes, unfortunately! Whatever is built has to break one day.

Questioner : The intense desire to experience marriage makes one forget his real Self (Soul). Where is the time for such thoughts of detachment in marriage?

Dadashri : However at that time, the thought occurred to me that whatever had begun, would eventually come to an end. Of the two of us, one of us would be widowed.

When you got married in the presence of all your guests and relatives, with the Sun and the priest as your witnesses, the *mantra* chanted by the priest was, *"Samaya varte savdhan,"* (Exercise caution according to the event in time). The priest understands what he is saying when he says, *"Samaya varte savdhan!"* but does the person getting married understand it? What does this *mantra* mean? It means that when your wife loses her temper, you should remain calm and alert. Only then, do you qualify for marriage. If she gets angry and you get angry too, then you have not exercised caution in time. When she gets upset, you should calm things down. Is it not necessary for you to be cautious? I had remained cautious. I never allowed any discord in my marriage. The moment any discord started, I would bring out the 'welding kit'.

Questioner : What is the root cause of all conflicts?

Dadashri : Tremendous ignorance. Men and women do not know how to live in this world. A man does not know how to be a father and neither does he know how to be a husband. Similarly, a woman does not know how to be a wife. They do not know the art of living. With all the material comforts, benefits, and conveniences, there is still so much misery. People live in the ocean of bliss and yet they are searching for a drop of water!

Questioner : But isn't quarrelling due to the differences in personality?

Dadashri : It is because of ignorance. In this world, no two personalities can ever match. After acquiring this understanding, there is only one solution, and that is, "Adjust everywhere".

God will not reside where there is conflict. So you can tell God, "Sir, you can stay in the temples, do not come to my home. We will construct more temples for you, but do not come to our home." God dwells where there is no strife. I guarantee you, God leaves as soon as quarrels arise and when that happens, people will tell me their business is not doing well. This is because God has departed. Your business will run smoothly as long as God is present. Do you enjoy quarrelling?

Questioner : No.

Dadashri : But it still occurs, doesn't it?

Questioner : Sometimes.

Dadashri : *Diwali* (Hindu religious festival) and Christmas also come sometimes. Do they come everyday?

Questioner : The quarrelling stops after fifteen minutes or so.

Dadashri : Remove all clashes from your life. Otherwise, you will lose your right to be a human being in your next life. Your human birth is the result of many good deeds in previous lives. To be of Indian lineage, is even a higher blessing. For all Indians here in the US and the UK, there is no shortage of material conveniences; there is pure, healthy food, which is further evidence of your *punyas* (merit *karma*) from your past life. What a tragedy it is if you waste all that away by bickering.

Our lives at home should be free of conflicts. We should be capable of at least this much. If the wife does not understand then you should explain to her, "If there are conflicts in our home, God will go away. So let's make a decision that we do not want any more quarrelling in our home." Having made this decision, if quarrelling still takes place, then understand that it is beyond your control. If she starts quarrelling, just go to bed. After a while, she too will go to sleep. But what if you argue back?

Why don't you make a decision not to quarrel for at least three days and see what happens. What is wrong with experimenting? Some people go on a fast for three days to improve their health, don't they? In the same way, try not to quarrel. Everyone at home should sit down together and decide, "I liked what Dada said, so from this moment on, we will not allow any quarrels to take place." Then just see what happens.

Questioner : Here, in America, even the women go out to work, so they feel a sense of power, and this leads to an increase in conflicts between husband and wife.

Dadashri : It is good if the women become a little powerful. We should take that positively; we should think it is good because now the 'cart' will run better. Is it better to have weak bullocks pulling the cart or powerful ones?

Questioner : If the power is used properly, then it is fine, but if that power were to be misused, then the cart would run poorly.

Dadashri : If there is no one to accept the effect of her power, then it will just bounce against the wall. If she uses that power and it does not perturb you, then all her power will bounce off the wall and come back to her. It will hurt her.

Questioner : Are you trying to tell us that we shouldn't listen to what they are saying?

Dadashri : Do listen. Listen to everything very carefully. It is beneficial for you to listen to everything, but if her power causes conflicts, then remain silent. You should just observe the degree to which her ego is intoxicated. The power she will exercise will be in proportion to the degree of intoxication.

Questioner : That is true. Similarly should we do the same when the men use their power unnecessarily?

Dadashri : That is when you have to exercise the same care. "Hmm, today he seems to be in a scolding mood…." You can tell yourself this in your mind, but do not say anything to his face.

Questioner : Yes, otherwise it will add fuel to the fire.

Dadashri : "There was a big blow up today," they will say. Things should not be this way. How beautiful a friendship can be between two friends! Can two friends behave in this manner? Would they still remain friends if they acted in this manner? Husband and wife are considered friends. Therefore they have to run their home like two friends would. You should not create problems. Is this why parents get their daughters married? Do they give their daughters to you so that you can behave in this manner? Is this behaviour becoming of you? What do you think? It does not suit us. Who do you call civilized? Is it the ones who have conflicts at home or the ones who have none?

There should not be even a single quarrel in the home, but if it happens to occur, you should solve it. As soon as you think the flames are going to ignite, throw water on it and cool it down. What is the advantage of living a life of quarrels? What is the meaning of it? There should be no quarrelling in life. What are you going to divide and take with you when you die? Why have quarrels when you have to eat and sleep together? You get upset when someone says anything negative about your husband, but you do not have any problems when you do the same. It should not be this way. Even the husband should not do this. Any quarrels you have, will affect your children's lives. Quarrels in the home affect the growing minds of children. Homes that are free of quarrels will have healthy children with emotional maturity. Otherwise a lot of problems will ensue for these children in the future.

Since the spontaneous expression of this *Gnan* within me twenty years ago and even twenty years prior to the *Gnan,* there has been no quarrelling in my home life. In this world, you cannot afford to quarrel under any circumstances.

So from now on, think before you do it. Otherwise take Dada Bhagwan's name. I too, take Dada Bhagwan's name before I do anything. As soon as you take Dada Bhagwan's name, your work will get done, as you would like it.

[3] DIFFERENCES OF OPINION BETWEEN HUSBAND AND WIFE

First and foremost, we need to get rid of anger, pride, attachment, greed, and reduce conflicts due to differences of opinions. This is our goal. We have to let the light of knowledge guide us. How long can you remain in the darkness? Have you seen the consequences of anger, pride, attachment, greed, and discord?

Questioner : Yes, many times.

Dadashri : Where, in the courtroom?

Questioner : At home, in the courts, discord exists everywhere.

Dadashri : What is the situation at home? There are only three of you at home, how can you have discord? You do not even have too many children. What possible reason for discord exists in your home of three people?

Questioner : There is a lot of discord even amongst the three of us.

Dadashri : Is that so? Even amongst the three of you?

Questioner : Life would not be fun if there were no conflicts!

Dadashri : Oh ho ho! Is this the kind of fun you look for? If so, then why don't you have conflicts everyday? Which smart Alec made this discovery?

Questioner : No Dada, we do not want that kind of fun.

Dadashri : All these people are simply rationalizing their irresponsible behaviour.

What is the cost of discord? Is it expensive or cheap? Do you have a lot of or a little discord?

Questioner : Sometimes there is less discord, sometimes more. It is expensive.

Dadashri : Some days you celebrate and some days you quarrel. Do you enjoy the quarrels, or does it ruin the fun?

Questioner : That is how the world revolves.

Dadashri : No, these are all excuses for people. Rather than admit their own weakness, they blame it on the world.

Questioner : It is definitely a weakness on our part, and that is why the problems occur.

Dadashri : Yes, that is it. People try to hide their weakness by saying this is how the world revolves. It is because they hide their weakness, that their weakness remains. What does the weakness say? It says, "Until you acknowledge my presence, I will not leave."

Questioner : But discord happens at home. Is it not part of life?

Dadashri : Our people fight every day and then they say, "This is what happens in a family." You fools! Such an attitude hinders progress. Why not investigate it? Why do such things happen? Why do you speak the way you do? Why do things the way they do? You have to investigate this.

Whenever you have discord in the home, what remedy do you use? Do you keep a bottle of medicine?

Questioner : There is no medicine for differences of opinions between a husband and a wife.

Dadashri : Eh? What are you saying? You are saying that you sit silently in one room, while she remains silent in another room. Do you go to sleep not speaking to each other? Do you not apply medication when you get hurt? How do you expect the wound to heal if you do not apply the medication? Explain to me how a wound can heal without being treated with medicine. That wound will not heal by the morning. Similarly, your wife will sulk as she serves you a cup of tea the next morning. Even you will find that the wound has not healed from the previous night. Does this happen or not? All this talk is not beyond anyone's experience. We are all the same! So why do you behave in a manner that does not let the wounds heal?

Unfortunately, day in and day out, those wounds remain. The gashes will not go away, they will be left behind. Therefore you should try to prevent these wounds from occurring. If you hurt her now, then in your old age, your wife will do the same to you. At the moment she will not say anything, she will think in her mind "He is very strong, so let him be." Later on however, when the time comes, she will take revenge. Therefore, you must conduct your interactions in such a manner that you will love each other. Everyone makes mistakes. What is the point of quarrelling when mistakes occur? If you want to fight, why don't you do it with someone more powerful and stronger, so that you will get your answer right away? Here you will never get your answer. Both of you should remember, "Dada has warned us about ruining our lives by quarrelling and creating discord."

Do not harbour any opinions, especially after marriage. Why should there be any differences of opinion after marriage? There will be no discord if you do not have an opinion. You both got married, so how can you afford to have opinions that are contrary?

Questioner : We should not, but it does happen.

Dadashri : So get rid of the differing opinions. Is it right for you to keep differences? If so, you shouldn't have married. Since you *did* marry, you both should become one.

You don't even know how to live life! You live a life filled with so many worries. Are you single? "No, I am married," one may say. So despite having a wife your worries have not stopped? Should your worries not be over? I have thought about this very deeply. Should everyone not think about this also? This world is so immense, yet these men believe that the whole world is (fits) within their room. They simply do not see how insignificant the fights within their home are, in comparison to the size of this world. Even if they were to believe that their room is their whole world, it would be fine but even there they dominate and bully their wives.

Questioner : If two utensils clash, there will be some noise, but eventually the noise will die down. Similarly, when two people clash, they will argue, but eventually the arguing will subside.

Dadashri : Your wife may say, "You do not have an ounce of common sense!" Are you pleased by such a statement?

Questioner : But then she also says, "I like no one but you."

Dadashri : Yes, she will say that too!

Questioner : But people living together are bound to argue.

Dadashri : How can you afford to accept arguments that occur every day? You have accepted this because you do not understand. Those who are aware of the real nature of this world would lose sleep even over a minor difference of opinion. Husbands and wives have vibrations. They emit vibrations even as they lay in bed thinking, "He is awkward, he is useless, he deserves to be thrown out!" Only living beings can emit vibrations. Those, which are not living, do not create vibrations. Without any understanding, people come to accept that discord is inevitable with married couples. You fool! Nobody has ever seen this Dada quarrel. Why all this noise? All this noise is ultimately harmful to only you. We ourselves are responsible for these conflicts. Is it ever someone else's responsibility? If you bang your fists on the dinning table because your tea is not ready, who is in danger? Instead it is better to remain sitting like a dummy! If you get your cup of tea, it is good and well, but, if you do not get it, then just go to work. What's wrong with doing that? Even a cup of tea has its timing does it not? Every event has a time and a place. This world is exact. Nothing happens outside the laws of nature. That is why I have said everything is *'vyavasthit'* (event that occurs as a result of countless scientific circumstantial evidences coming together). When the time comes for you to get your tea, you will get your tea, regardless of your temper tantrums. You do not need to bang on anything. Your tea will be ready and waiting for you whether you create negative vibrations or not. But by creating vibrations you will add to your account (karmic) and some day she will remind you, of the day that you were banging your fists on the table.

People do not have the ability to solve problems with their spouses or their children and when clashes occur they fall deeper into confusion.

Questioner : The husband believes that it is his wife who must compromise, and not him.

Dadashri : Yes that means the limit has been reached. If the wife has to compromise and he won't, it means that things have come to head. A *gentleman* on the other hand, would speak in a manner that would make his wife happy. *He* would move forward in this way, but *you* conduct yourself in such a way that your situation stagnates for weeks and months on end. Nothing gets resolved. Unless there is closure in the mind of the opposing party, you will have difficulties. Therefore, you must compromise.

How can you accept this discord at home? When the wife says, "I am yours," and the husband says, "I am yours," where is there room for any discord? As problems between the two of you increase, a separation between you will begin. There is pain in separation. Everyone has problems, not just you. Anyone who gets married will have such problems. But after these problems are solved, you will not feel a mental separation. Any sense of separation causes pain.

How can you have problems with your wife? A person with whom... Do you have a double bed or a single?

Questioner : No please forgive me. We only have one bed.

Dadashri : Then if you quarrel with her, what will you do if she kicks you out of the bed?

Questioner : I would sleep on the floor.

Dadashri : So keep oneness with her. If you quarrel with your wife, and if you don't keep oneness with her, then with whom else will you maintain oneness with? What does 'oneness' mean? It means never to have discord. This is the one person with whom you must decide not to have discord with. You need to keep that much oneness. Have you ever kept this kind of oneness?

Questioner : I have never thought like this before. This is the first time I am thinking.

Dadashri : Yes, you will have to think, won't you? God too, did so much thinking and then attained *moksha*.

Talk to me! Let's discuss everything so that you can acquire solutions to your problems. It is due to a favorable opportunity that you are here in front of me, so talk to me. Do you have any objection to that? We all are one, but it is because of your intellect that you feel a sense of separation. Your intellect makes you perceive separation, but in reality, everything is one. Humans have intellect that enables them to discriminate. Is this intellect in operation where your wife is concerned?

Questioner : Yes that is what happens.

Dadashri : What causes this sense of separation with your wife? The intellect causes it.

When a man and his wife both fight with a neighbour, they unite against the neighbour. When you see both of them raise their fists at the neighbour, you think, "Wow what unity, what oneness! This couple is united." However, when they go back inside the house and they themselves fight, the husband will say to his wife, "Go back to your parent's home, I do not want you at all!" Now is there any understanding here? What do you think? The two were united earlier, but that unity breaks down and the separation between them begins. Now, even with his own wife, he starts using words like, 'mine' and 'yours'. He accuses her, "You're like this, and you're like that." She responds by asking, "When have you ever been straight?" So even in your own home everything becomes 'mine' and 'yours'.

Couples now separate themselves by saying, "Me and you, me and you, me and you!" whereas in the past, they used to refer to themselves as 'us'. "'We' two, are one, 'we' are like this and 'we' are like that. It is 'ours.'" The word 'we' and 'ours', turn into 'mine' and 'yours', initiating quarrels and rivalry. At what point will these quarrels end? Divorce and devastation are the results. These quarrels destroy everything. So do not get into conflict with anyone.

Day after day the husband will say "My wife, my wife," but, if they are going out of town and the wife happens to pack one of her *saris* in his suitcase, he will start yelling, "Why have you packed your *sari* in my bag?" Just observe the behaviour of these so-called 'reputable' men! Was her *sari* going to eat him up? He behaves in this manner because he claims a separate identity. This 'husband-wife' relationship is a type of business; it is the reason they get together. It is a contract. Will they lose their separate identities? No, that identity remains separate only. Does he not ask, "Why did you pack your *saris* in my bag?"

Questioner : Yes, he does.

Dadashri : These men argue over a simple *sari*. The wife thinks to herself, "He always creates this problem, even if I touch his bag. I must have made a mistake about him when I was looking for a husband. From where did I get such a husband?" But what can she do now? She is dependent upon him. She has no option left. If it were a woman from the western world, she would have left him the very next day. But how can an Indian lady leave, when she is tied and bound? There is no place for fighting. If there was, they would definitely kill each other!

There are some men who are so petty that they make their wives move their bag if it happens to be standing next to theirs! You fool! You are a married man and you went through a marriage ceremony. Have you not both become one? The husband even refers to his wife as his 'other half'. What kind of a man are you? Why do you refer to her as your 'other half'? Does this 'other half' not apply to your bags also? Who are we ridiculing, the men or the women? Do people not use the term 'my other half'?

Questioner : They do.

Dadashri : Then they change their minds. The women don't cause such problems. If he were to pack his jeans in her bag, she wouldn't say anything. But these men have such big egos; their ego is always poised to strike upon the slightest of irritation, just like a scorpion. Keep in mind I am telling you this from my own past experiences so that you too can understand what I have experienced. By hearing this, you will also get the strength to accept your errors. Otherwise you are not likely to admit them easily.

Questioner : Yes Dada, when you say this, everyone remembers their own past and they accept their mistakes.

Dadashri : No, you would not accept it, but I will admit that I have experienced them all. Men hurt their wives so much. They will things that really sting; they will tell them to go back to their parent's house. Foolish man! What would become of you, if she were to leave? She is bound to you through *karma,* so where can that poor lady go? What you are telling her will not go to waste. Instead it will leave a wound on her heart, and then come back to you later you fool. You will have to suffer the effect of this *karma.* You might think to yourself, "Where would she go? You must never say such things. It is a very grave mistake if you do. All you men here have used such taunts sometime or the other, have you not?

Questioner : Yes, we have. Everyone has done it. There are no exceptions. The intensity of the taunts may be different, but there are no exceptions.

Dadashri : So this is what everything is like. Now tell me, I have to make all these men wise! How will they become wise? They move about with frowns on their faces; they look as if they just drank some castor oil. They eat such delicious meals cooked by their wives, and yet their faces look like they just drank some castor oil.

Questioner : What should one do to get rid of discord at home?

Dadashri : First investigate what causes the discord. If you have a son and a daughter, do you ever disagree about the fact that both of them are not sons?

Questioner : No, the differences occur over very trivial matters.

Dadashri : Oh in these trivial matters, it is simply egoism at fault. If she says something, you should say, "That is fine." That is the end of it. But instead, you use your intellect, which then clashes with the other intellect, causing discord.

Questioner : What should I do to be able to say, "That is okay," to my wife? I am not able to say that. How can I keep away from this ego?

Dadashri : You are right it is not easily done. To remedy that, you have to practice doing it for a few days. For a few days, practice what I am saying, and then it will happen. It will not happen immediately.

Questioner : What is the reason behind this discord?

Dadashri : The differences occur because the husband thinks he is intelligent and the wife thinks she is intelligent. Here come two bags full of intelligence! You wouldn't even get a dime if you were to sell these bags! Instead, be aware and observe her intelligence...oh my! How intelligent she is! That way even she will calm down. But if you exercise your intellect and she does the same, there will be a fight.

Who experiences more discord, you or her?

Questioner : She is the one who gets upset more.

Dadashri : What is discord? Let me explain. Have you ever played the game of tug-of-war?

Questioner : Yes.

Dadashri : Two teams of players will pull a rope at opposite ends. Conflict is synonymous to a game of tug-of-war. What will happen if you both are pulling strongly at opposite ends?

Questioner : It will break.

Dadashri : If it breaks, you will have to tie a knot in it. Instead of having to tie a knot, what is wrong with simply leaving the rope intact? If she pulls hard, you should just let go.

Questioner : But of the two, who should be the first to let go?

Dadashri : The one who has understanding. The one who has the right understanding will let go and the one who is using the wrong intellect will continue pulling. But when you let go, do not let go all of a sudden, because if you do, she will fall. Let go very gradually, otherwise the poor person on the opposing end, will fall down. So from now on, will you let go of this rope? Let go, otherwise you will have to tie a knot in it and then use it. Does it look good to tie knots in it every day? You have to use that rope again! What do you think?

Do you have discord at home? It should not occur at all. If it happens then you are an unfit husband, and if the wife does it, then she is an unfit wife.

Questioner : How do quarrels between a husband and wife, affect their children?

Dadashri : Oh ho! Quarrels have very negative effects indeed! A small child watches his dad abusing his mother. He will think that the father is the culprit, but he dare not say anything. He knows that if he says anything he will be punished. These children make a note of everything. When they see such trouble in the house, they make a mental note to themselves, "When I grow up, I will sort out my father!" He will then grow up and abuse his dad! The dad will say, "Did I bring you up so that you could beat me?" The son will say, "Then who brought you up?" The father will retort, "Are you bringing my father into this?" and the son will reply, "I will even bring in your grandfather!" He does this, because his father gave him the scope to do so. It is our own fault as parents that we spoil their minds by quarrelling. Why should we fight at home? If parents do not fight, children will not make note of this, and they will grow up respecting their parents.

Why are young adults and teenagers disenchanted about marriage? I asked them what objection they had. "Is it that you don't like women, that you don't like being with a woman or is it because you are not a man? Why? What is the reasoning for you opposition to marriage?" They say they have not witnessed happiness in a marriage. I ask them how they know this when they are still so young and unmarried. They reply, "We have seen the so-called 'happiness' of our parents. We have seen their misery. If we get married, then we too, will be miserable." Does that happen?

Suppose I tell you it is dark outside, but this man disagrees, and says it is still light outside. I would tell him to look again. If he still insists that it is daylight, I would realize that his statement was based on his perception. Because one does not have the ability to go beyond his perception, I would tell him that he is correct by his viewpoint. I would simply say, "Yes, you are correct by your viewpoint," and then I will move on. Why would I waste time with him unnecessarily? He is not going to change. This is the way to bring an end to discord.

Imagine that there is a beautiful white horse standing about five hundred feet from here. We show it to everyone and ask them what they see. Someone may say it is a cow. Now what can we do about that? Should we punish him?

Questioner : No.

Dadashri : Why not?

Questioner : According to his vision, he sees a cow.

Dadashri : Yes…his spectacles are like that. We should realize that the poor man has a different perception. It is not his fault and therefore, we cannot get upset with him. Just tell him that he is right and ask someone else what he sees. We must simply understand that people's beliefs are based upon their perceptions. Those who see differently, have a different perception. What do you think?

I have been married for fifty-five years. I made mistakes up until the age of twenty-five or thirty. Before *Gnan,* when I was young, I too, used to throw things in anger. I had an ego! The ego of a reputable Patel from the six villages! The high and mighty! Then one day, I realized that my nobility was lost in the act of throwing things in anger. My reputation was auctioned in such acts. Do our (Indian) men throw things at women? These bags of ignorance! Is this a becoming conduct for us? Does this suit us?

Questioner : At least when you throw things it is over and done with. But when you gain possession of internal differences, its results are much worse, because they cause one to continually behave differently. Is that not considered more dangerous?

Dadashri : Internal differences? Those are extremely dangerous.

I have searched through scriptures and for a solution to these internal differences. I did not find anything in any of the scriptures. Then, I discovered the solution myself, and that was to rid myself of my own opinions, to get rid of my opinions, in order to prevent conflicts with others. Where there are no opinions, there is no scope for conflict.

Your opinion is my opinion.

Once I had a conflict with Hiraba. Even I became trapped in a difficult situation. I used to call my wife, 'Hiraba'. As a *Gnani Purush,* I can either address women as, *'Ba'* (mother: gesture of respect towards elderly ladies) or as *'dikri'* (daughter). If you are interested, I can tell you. It is not a long story, just a short one.

Questioner : Yes, do tell us.

Dadashri : One day we had a conflict of opinions

("conflict" or "difference of opinion"). The mistake was mine; Hiraba was not at fault.

Questioner : She may have made the mistake, but you claim it was yours.

Dadashri : Yes, but it was not her mistake, it was mine. I am the one who does not want any conflict. She did not care whether a conflict took place or not and because I did, it is considered my mistake. If I do this (Dada hits the chair), does the chair get hurt or do I get hurt?

Questioner : You.

Dadashri : Therefore, it is up to me to understand.

So anyway, one day there was a conflict and I got trapped. Hiraba told me that her brother's eldest daughter was getting married and then asked me what we should give her as a gift. It would have been fine if she had not asked me. Whatever she wanted to give her would have been just fine and I would not have objected. However, when she asked me, I responded according to my intellect and said, "Rather than having new silverware made, why don't you take one or two pieces of the silverware we have in the cupboard and give them as a gift?" Do you know what her reply was? In our house words like 'mine' and 'yours' are never used. Only the words 'our' or 'ours' are used. So she said, "When your uncle's son got married, you gave huge silver plates." Now on that day, she used the words 'mine' and 'yours,' when normally she would say 'ours.' She would never make the separation of 'mine' and 'yours'. This was the first time. I thought to myself, "Today I am trapped!" I realized my mistake instantly, and looked for an opportunity to get out of the predicament. Now, how could I mend this damage? The bleeding had already started, so how could I apply the bandage in order to stop the bleeding?

So on that day 'mine' and 'yours' took place. The situation went so far, that she used the words, "*Your* uncle's son," rather than "*Our* nephew." I realized that I had made a major mistake. That day I saw that I was about to take a fall, so I immediately corrected myself. I lied. It is better to do that, than to create discord. I turned the situation around quickly and completely. I told her, "I did not mean to say that! I am trying to say something else. There is a little misunderstanding on your part. I am not saying that." Then when she asked me what I was trying to say, I replied, "Give her the silverware in addition to five hundred rupees. She could use the money!" In turn she replied, "You are so naive, how can you give so much?" At that point, I realized I had won over the situation. So then I told her, "You can give whatever you want to. All four of your nieces are like our own daughters." At that point she became content! "You are truly divine," she said.

You see I fixed the damage. I knew that if I had said five hundred rupees, she was not likely to give that much. I passed on the responsibility to her. I knew her nature. If I gave her five hundred rupees, she would give only three hundred. So tell me why would I have a problem in giving her the authority?

[4] NAGGING AT MEAL-TIMES

Why do you interfere in household matters? Don't people make mistakes? Who is likely to make mistakes, those who work or those who do not do anything?

Questioner : The ones who work.

Dadashri : So do not point out any mistakes in her cooking. If the *kadhee* (soup dish made from yoghurt) is too salty, you don't have to comment on it. Put aside what you do not like and eat the rest. Men have a habit of pointing out their wives mistakes and telling them off. Men have developed that habit. However, these ladies are no angels either. Nowadays, family life is synonymous to the cold war between America and Russia; it has become "America versus Russia". That is why I make you understand how to live like a family. These conflicts go on in every household.

If the food is not to your liking, can you not refrain from making a comment? If there is too much salt in the *kadhee,* can you not refrain from saying anything? Don't you think she will realize it herself? Is it necessary for you to comment about it? And even when you have guests for dinner, you don't let them dine peacefully. Now why should you do such a thing? When she tastes the food herself, she will find out, without you blowing your horn.

Questioner : But if the *khadee* is salty, then you have to say it is salty.

Dadashri : Then your life too, will become salty. You are insulting her by telling her it is too salty. That is not being a family.

Questioner : You can say it to your own people, but you cannot say it to others, can you?

Dadashri : So you can abuse your own?

Questioner : If you tell her, she would be sure do a better job the next time.

Dadashri : Whether she does a good job or not, such comments are not needed. Why do such things happen? It is neither under the control of the maker nor is it under the control of the person who comments on the food. Under whose control is all this? I know the cause behind everything.

Have you become a little wiser? You will be, won't you? You have to become absolutely wise. Your wife should say, "I want a husband like you in every life." A lady once told me, "Dada, if I have to have a husband, I would like this very same one every time." So far, she is the only one who has said this to me. I remember her.

You cannot play games with women. Why do you have to criticize her cooking? Why do you have to comment if the vegetables get cold or if the *daal* does not have the right spices? Why do you keep on nagging in this manner? If you speak in this manner once a year, then it is okay, but why do so everyday? Whether the *daal* is bad or the vegetables are too cold, it is all dependant upon the laws of nature. If it happens frequently, then you may want to say calmly, "These vegetables taste good when they are hot." When you say it in this way, she will get the hint.

Nobody at my home knows 'Dada's' likes and dislikes. Do you think the preparations and the cooking of a meal are under the control of the person cooking it? It all comes together on a plate by what *vyavasthit shakti* (scientific circumstantial evidences, the natural force) dictates for the one receiving it. You should not interfere in this.

[5] NEED A HUSBAND, NOT A BOSS

There is nothing wrong in looking at her closely before marrying her. You can look, provided she is going to remain the same her whole life. Will she remain the same as the day you first saw her? Would she not change? And when she changes, you will not be able to handle it; you will feel suffocated. Then where will you go? You have entered a trap.

Why get married? The reason for marriage is so that you can go out and work for money while she works at home. In this way, your married life proceeds well and you can practice religion. If she wants a couple of children, go ahead and settle that problem, and then after that delve into the higher aspects of life. Instead what do you do? You insist on being her boss. You silly man, why are you trying to become a boss?

Questioner : But why can't the wife take care of everything for me?

Dadashri : Oh ho! The wife exists to take care of all your needs?

Questioner : That is why we have brought home a wife.

Dadashri : Scriptures have proclaimed that a husband should not exercise any kind of dominance over his wife. You are not the boss. Your marriage is a partnership. In the worldly language, people use the terms "husband and wife," or "head of the household (husband)," implying that the wife is subordinate. Because it is a partnership, you do not have any ownership over your wife. You cannot make demands on her. You have to explain things to her in order to get your work done.

Questioner : In our wedding ceremony, the bride's parents perform the ritual of *kanyadaan* (*kanya:* unmarried girl; *daan:* gift, donation) in which they give the bride as a gift. Does that not make us their owners?

Dadashri : That is not for the civilized community. That is for the uncivilized community. In our civilized community, men should take every care to make sure that the wife does not suffer. Otherwise, they will never be happy. Just as no man has ever been happy by making his wife miserable, no woman who has made husband miserable has been happy either.

It is because of this dominating attitude and feeling of superiority that he gets out of hand and as a result, he will have to endure the consequences of his actions. It is nothing but suffering. With your wife, you have a partnership, not an ownership.

Questioner : What about the wife who becomes bossy?

Dadashri : That doesn't matter. She cooks good meals and feeds you. You have to say to her, "Oh my! You cook such wonderful meals for me!" That will please her and then she will calm down. You don't have to be afraid of her. When will she become your superior, when she grows a moustache? Is she ever likely to grow one?

Besides you only have one lifetime worth of accounts to settle. That account is not going to increase. So why not live in a peaceful manner?

Hindus, by nature, are volatile and that is why it is said that Hindus go through life, clashing with others. Muslims on the other hand, are very insightful; they conduct their fighting outside their homes, but at home they do not fight with their wives. Nowadays, we see the Muslims behaving like the Hindus, because they have close contact with them. But compared to the Hindus, I find them wiser in these matters. Some Muslims even pamper their wives by pushing them lovingly as they sit on the swings.

Questioner : Dada, why don't you tell us more about that incident of that Muslim gentleman and the swing?

Dadashri : Yes. One day I had gone to visit a Muslim friend. We were sitting on chairs and his wife was sitting on a swing. He got up and started to push the swing for his wife, so I inquired, "Does she not take advantage of you if you pamper her in this way?" He replied, "What advantage is she going to take? She does not have any weapons or anything of that sort!" I replied back, "Our Hindu men would never do this because

they are scared their wives may start taking advantage of them."
He then asked me if I knew the reason he pushed her on the
swing.

Between the years of 1943 and 1944, I had a
construction contract with the government. We had a Muslim
contract labourer by the name of 'Ahmedmiya'. He was our
head bricklayer. He had invited me several times to his home.
"Sahib, visit my little hut," he would say. Muslim people are soft
spoken and sincere, and although their conduct may or may not
correspond, they are pleasant and sincere when they speak.
One day he asked me if I would bless him by visiting his home,
and that it would make his wife and children very happy. I had
not yet received *Gnan* at that time, but my world vision was
very elevated. I had compassion for everyone. If I employed
someone, my inner intent was to always look out for their
welfare. I always wanted people to be free of their miseries and
become happy; such was my intent.

I had seen the good qualities of this (Muslim) community.
I agreed to visit him. He told me that he had only one room and
was concerned about where we would sit. I told him, "I will sit
anywhere, all I need is a chair and if you don't have any, then
I will do without one. But I will definitely come to your home.
It is your wish, so I will come." And so, I went. Because of my
business I frequently visited Muslim homes. I would also drink
tea at their homes. I did not hold any differences.

He had only two rooms, one large room and the other as
small as a bathroom. When I asked him about the rooms, he
replied, "Sir, what can I do? This is more than enough for us
poor people." I then asked him where his wife slept. He said,
"In this same room. You can call this a bedroom and a dinning
room, this room is everything." So I asked, "Ahmedmiya, don't
you ever fight with your wife?" He was amazed, "What are you

asking? That never happens. I am not a foolish man." "You must have a little discord?" I inquired. "Not with my wife," he replied. I went on, "What if your wife gets angry sometimes?" He replied, "I say to her, 'Beloved, outside that boss harasses me, and if you harass me here, what will become of me?' and she in turn, calms down." I replied, "Since there is no discord, there is no problem." He then replied by asking me what would happen if there *was* discord. He asked, "Where would *she* sleep and where would *I* sleep? If this home had three levels, then I could go away to the third floor. But here, we both have to sleep in the same room. She faces one wall and I face the other wall, what fun is there in that? The whole night we would not be able to sleep, and where else would I go? This is why I do not make my wife unhappy at all, even if she were to beat me up. I fight with everyone outside the home, but not with my wife. You cannot do anything to your wife. If I get angry, I go and fight outside, but not at home."

Let me offer another example. When Salia's wife (a Muslim family) asked him to buy meat, it was a dilemma. Since his wages were very minimal, how could the poor man afford to buy any meat? His wife had been telling him for over a month, that their poor children keep asking for mutton. Then one day the wife gets irritated, so he tells her he will bring some meat that evening. He is always prepared with answers, because if he is not, she continues to nag at him. Upon her irritation, he immediately gave her a positive reply. "I will bring it today, I will bring it from wherever I have to," he said. By saying this he prevented a quarrel. Thinking that he would bring meat home that day, as he had said, she became furious and started yelling, when he walked in empty-handed. Being the shrewd man that he is, Salia was able to pacify his wife by saying, "Dear heart, only I know my problems, you would not understand." In the same manner, Salia uttered a few more sentences and turned his wife around. Rather than continuing to yell, she told him that he could bring the meat another time, and not worry. After fifteen days or so, the same scenario occurred again, and again he pleaded his condition to her, making her happy in the end. By dealing with these situations in such a way, he never has to fight.

Hindu men on the other hand, would say, "You are trying to control me." You cannot say such a thing to your wife, these very words you utter, show that you are under control. You are being controlled. How can she control you? When even at the time of marriage, your hand was on top of hers, how can she control you? And if sometimes she ever controls you, just remain calm. Only the weak get irritated.

In Aurangabad, a Muslim man, about 25 years old, came to my *satsang*. He had heard from someone that he could receive spiritual knowledge from me. Upon hearing this, he came to listen to the *satsang*. I talked to him about this world and the soul. I explained the science to him. He liked the scientific approach and felt it was worth listening to. Until now whatever has been written has been a description of events of the time it was written. However, as the time changes, the description becomes more elaborate. What is the meaning of *'Paigambar'*? A *'Paigambar'* is the one, who brings God's *'paigaam'* (message) and makes it available for everyone. So I started to joke with him a little, and I asked him if he was married or just dating? He said he was married. Jokingly, I asked, "When? You didn't invite me?" "Dadaji," he replied, "I didn't know you, or I would have invited you the same day. I have been married only six months now." I was just teasing him. I asked him how many times he did *namaj* (Islamic prayer ritual). "Sir, I do it 5 times," he said. I then asked, "How are you able to do *namaj* at 3 o'clock in the morning?" He replied, "It has to be done, there is no choice. I have to get up at 3 o'clock and do it also." I asked him if his wife allowed him to do it at 3 o'clock in the morning. He replied, "Even as a young child I used to do it. My father, the doctor, he too used to do it." So I asked him, "Now that you have a wife, how does she let you do it at 3 o'clock?" He replied, "My wife too tells me that I have to do *namaj*." Then I asked him if he ever quarrelled with his wife. He was astonished, "What are you asking? What is this you ask? My wife is the sweetness of my life. If she tells me off, I accept it. Sir, it is because of my wife that I live. She gives me a lot of happiness. She makes wonderful meals and feeds me. How can I hurt her?" Now if men understood even this much, it would be good, they would not try to dominate your wife. Should they not understand this? Is the wife at fault? 'Sweetness of my life, even if she curses me, there is no problem. If anyone else was to curse at me, I would sort him out!' Now tell me how much these men cherish their wives!

[6] THE HABIT OF POINTING OUT FAULTS IN OTHERS

Questioner : She feels bad if her faults are pointed out to her, but she also feels bad if I do not say anything.

Dadashri : No, no, no, she will not feel bad. If you *do not* point out her mistakes, she will tell you herself that the *kadhee* was salty and she will ask you why you did not say something. That is when you tell her that you do not have to say anything because she would have found out eventually. Instead, you complain, "This soup is too salty!" which is accompanied by a look of disgust on your face. You foolish man! What kind of a man are you? How can one keep you as a husband? Such husbands need to be thrown out! Such weak husbands! Is she not able to see her mistakes herself that you have to create a conflict? Why hurt her unnecessarily? She will think to herself, "Don't you think I know that? You always criticize me. You hurt me all the time." Our people (Indian people) deliberately point out minor and obvious mistakes, and that is why their lives are so full of clashes. What do you think? Do you have any objection to thinking a little on this point?

Questioner : If we point out her mistakes, then she will not make the same mistake again will she?

Dadashri : Oh ho! You want a reason to preach! Yes, there is nothing wrong in pointing out her mistakes. What I am telling you is that you can only do so, if she appreciates you telling her. If she tells you, "It's a good thing you pointed out my mistake, I was not aware of it," then it is okay for you to do so. Tell me dear, do you appreciate it when he points out your mistakes?

Questioner : No.

Dadashri : What is the point in showing her the mistake she is already aware of? If there is something wrong with the cooking will she not know when she eats the meal herself? So there is no need for you to say anything. If she was not aware of her mistake and you were to point it out to her, she may appreciate it. Only Indian men do this.

When I lived on the third floor in Santa Cruz in Bombay, tea used to be brought up to me. Some days they would forget to put sugar in the tea. I would drink the tea telling Dada within, "Sahib, put some sugar in this tea," and He would. I would drink the tea even if there were no sugar in it. Interference was not my nature. Later on, everyone would be rushing around to bring the sugar. I would ask them, "Why did you bring sugar?" They in turn, would ask, "Why did you not ask for sugar, the tea was not sweet?" I would reply, "Why do I need to tell you?" Do you understand what I am saying?

I asked one man if he ever pointed out his wife's

mistakes. He said she was full of mistakes so he needed to point them out to her. I told him, "You klutz! You bundle of intelligence! If you were to sell this bundle, no one would give you even ten cents in return. And here you think your wife is full of mistakes!"

Questioner : People are often aware of their mistakes but what if they do not improve. What then?

Dadashri : They cannot improve by you telling them. On the contrary, they get worse. It is only when they think about their mistakes, that you can talk to them directly about how they can improve. Communicate openly with her, like you would with a friend. Should you not have a friendship with your wife? You keep friendship with others. Do you argue with your friends daily in this manner? Do you openly point out their mistakes to them? No! That is because you want to keep that friendship. Whereas with your wife you think, "Where can she go, now that she is married?" This kind of behaviour does not suite us. Make your life like a garden. Your home should feel like you are in a garden. You should not let any problems occur for anyone in the home. The same applies with your children; if they are aware of their mistakes then you should not point them out to them. You can only show them the mistakes they are not aware of.

It is sheer lunacy to exercise dominance as a husband. What is the sign of being a good husband? It is when you do not meet any opposition from your wife. But here there is opposition all the time.

Everyone nags at the woman in the home. That is not a sign of gallantry. Gallant is the man who does not cause any difficulty for his wife or his children in the home. The child may talk back, but if the parents remain unperturbed, that is a real partnership. That is called a real marriage. Children are innocent, naïve, and immature. What do you think? What does justice tell you?

Draw attention to only the faults they are not aware of or cannot see for themselves. If you nag them about their mistakes they already know of, you will hurt their ego. They will then wait for a chance to repay you. They wait for that opportunity. What is the need for this? There is no need to call their attention to things they already understand.

If it (your problem) is too bitter, then you should swallow it alone, how can you allow the women to drink it? After all we are *Mahadevji* (Lord Mahadev symbolizes a being that can swallow all the poisons and bitterness of the world without any complaints or retaliation). Are we not *Mahadevji*? Men are like *Mahadevji*. If the situation gets too much, you can tell her, "You don't worry, you go to sleep, I'll take care of it." Don't the poor ladies give us a lot of support in life? So then how can we afford to have problems with them? If you hurt her in any way, then you should repent for it secretly. Tell her, "From now on, I will not hurt you. I made a mistake. Please forgive me."

What kinds of hurt take place in your home? What kind of arguments? What kind of discord? If you both write all this down on a paper and bring it to me, I will solve them all for you in an hour. They occur because of misunderstanding, nothing else.

All the problems of the home should stay within the four walls of your home. This is how you should live together as a family. If you make just this much of a change, it is very good. There should be absolutely no quarrelling. You should live within your means. If you do not have enough money, then you should not be in a hurry to buy *saris*. You should be conscious of not putting your husband in a financial difficulty. Spend only if you have the money.

[7] OVERHEATED RADIATOR OF A CAR

If sometimes the husband comes home late because of some unavoidable circumstances, the wife will comment, "Huh! Why did you come home so late?" Does she not realize that he knows he is late? He is already feeling uncomfortable about being late and then on top of that she has to nag him about it. The poor man! Talking this way is meaningless. Do you understand all this? So if he comes home late some day, then you have to see what kind of a mood he is in. If he is not in a good mood, give him a nice cup of tea and put him in a good mood before he sits down to dinner. Don't you offer a cup of tea to a policeman, if he comes to your house, even if you are not in a good mood? This is your own husband, shouldn't you please him? He is your own so you have to make him happy. Many of you know what happens when a car gets overheated. Do we hit it with a stick or do we come up with ways to cool the radiator? Similarly you have to cool the 'radiator'; you have to turn on the fan. Can you not do that?

Questioner : How can I stop him from drinking so much brandy?

Dadashri : When he sees love in your home he will stop everything. He is ready to stop anything for love. When he does not see love at home, he falls in love with the brandy. He will fall in love with something or other. He will wander around on the beach all day. You foolish man, what are you are going to find on the beach, go home, why don't you? But he will say, "But I don't like it at home."

[8] SHOULD YOU IMPROVE OTHERS OR YOURSELF?

All these relationships are relative and temporary. Many husbands become so obsessed in trying to improve their wives, that it destroys the love between them. He thinks he has to improve her. You fool, why don't you improve yourself? Improve just once. Besides, she is not yours permanently. She will leave you when she leaves this world. One day your relationship will end. This is just temporary, so take care of her, come to an agreement with her and enjoy her company in harmony.

Questioner : *Prakruti* (a person's inherent characteristics, tendencies, personality etc.) cannot be improved, but shouldn't our worldly interactions improve?

Dadashri : People do not understand the nature of worldly interactions. If people knew how to interact for just half an hour, it would be more than enough. What is the definition of 'worldly interaction'? It is to remain superficial. Understand that the worldly life is not the absolute reality; people believe this world to be the ultimate truth and reality. The truth of this world is a relative truth; it is all relative and temporary. Right worldly interaction does not mean insisting on the truth. People believe that insistence on the truth is the right worldly interaction. This type of behaviour is of no importance when it comes to salvation and real freedom. Stop fretting and get your work done. Worldly interaction means paying back what was taken and taking back what you had given. If someone says you do not have any sense, you should realize that it is time for you to pay back what you had given to him in the past life. Understanding this principle is called the right or correct worldly interaction. At the moment nobody has the correct worldly interaction. The one, who understands worldly interaction as being worldly in nature (temporary), is truly free.

Someone may tell you, "Straighten out your wife!" but if you try to straighten her, you yourself will become crooked. Therefore, don't try to straighten her. Accept her the way she is. It is a different matter if you have a permanent relationship with her, but after this one life, she will be away somewhere, with someone else. You both have different timings of death, you both have different karma, nothing can be given or taken and nothing can be changed. Where she will go from here, who knows? You may straighten her up and she will end up going to someone else in the next life.

Only he who has improved himself can improve others. *Prakruti* cannot change, nor can it be controlled by threats. It is because of all such threats that these worldly problems continue. *Prakruti* worsens with threats.

If you are really concerned about improving your spouse, do not quarrel or create conflicts with her. Some hard-headed person will come along for her improvement.

How can you destroy someone who is under your protection? Your highest aim should be to protect her even if she is at fault. See how these Pakistani prisoners are protected, despite being prisoners here? Whereas this is your wife, is she not your own? Outside the home, men become cowards, but at home they fight.

[9] ADJUST EVERYWHERE THROUGH COMMON SENSE

There is no difference between colliding into a wall and arguing over a difference of opinion with someone. It is essentially the same thing. A person bumps into a wall because he cannot see and a person gets into conflict because he cannot see. One cannot see what lies ahead of him, and the other cannot see a solution ahead of him, so he gets into arguments. All these enemies of anger, pride, attachment, and greed arise because of our inability to see what lies ahead. This is how we should understand everything. It is not the fault of the wall; it is the fault of the person who is hurt by it. All these (people) are walls as such. All conflicts are like bumping into a wall. When you bump into a wall you do not at who is at fault do you? You don't try to prove that you were right, do you?

You must think of everyone that clashes with you, as being a wall. Look for the door, so even in the darkness you will be able to find your way out. You need to make it a rule not to clash with anyone.

[10] TWO SEPARATE DEPARTMENTS

Men should not interfere in women's affairs and women should not interfere with men's affairs. Each should stay within his or her departments.

Questioner : What is a woman's department? What matters should men not interfere in?

Dadashri : Cooking and running the household is a woman's department. It is not necessary for the husband to know where she buys her groceries and her grains. If she tells you she is having problems trying to get some grains, then it is a different matter. Is there any need to interfere in her department when she does not ask for your help? There is no need to tell her what to cook either. When the time comes, your meal will be served. Her department is her territory. If some day you have an intense desire to eat something, then you can ask her to cook it for you. I am not telling you that you cannot say anything, however when you complain about things as trivial as the soup being too salty, you are interfering in her department.

A good husband will not interfere in the domestic affairs of his wife. If he does, he is like a woman. There are some men who go into the kitchen and check the spice containers to see how much have been used up in the last two months. You fool, where will it all end if you start doing this? That is a concern for the person who runs that department. Things get used up and have to be replaced. But why are you trying to be a 'smart Alec'? You should not interfere in her kitchen department.

In the first few years of our marriage there was some interference. Then gradually we cleaned up all the mess and made a decision that the kitchen and the running of the household were her responsibility and earning money was mine. We were not to interfere in each other's affairs.

If you see the interaction in our home, you would find it very pleasant. When Hiraba was healthy, she would personally go to the vegetable stand at the end of our street to buy vegetables. If I were home she would ask me what vegetables she should bring. I would tell her to bring whatever she wanted to. Then she would go out and buy them. This is how it would go on everyday, so what would one do in this situation? She then stopped asking me and it went on this way for a few days, so one day I asked her, "Why did you bring these *karelas* (bitter gourds)?" She replied, "Whenever I ask you what I should bring, you tell me I should buy whatever I want, and now you're pointing out my mistakes?" I replied, "No, we have to keep a practice where you ask me what vegetables to buy and I tell you whatever you feel like. Keep this custom of ours going!" This custom she carried out till the end. Even the people who came to visit us were impressed. How wonderful was the custom of this household! Therefore your worldly dealings should look good on the outside. It should not be one-sided. How wise Lord Mahavir was! He kept the real and the relative separate. Not one-sided at all. Don't people make note of worldly interactions? People saw us everyday. "Does she ask you this everyday?" my friends would ask. Then when I told them yes, they asked, "Doesn't she get tired?" they asked. I in turn asked, "Why would she get tired? It is not as if she has to climb a bunch or stairs or a mountain." Conduct your worldly interaction in a manner, which people appreciate.

Questioner : In which matters should a wife not interfere in her husband's affairs?

Dadashri : She must not interfere in *any* of her husband's affairs. "How much merchandise came into the shop today? How much merchandise did you sell? Why did you come late?" The husband would then have to say, "I missed the nine o'clock train!" Then she would question, "What were you doing that you missed the train?" which causes him to become irritated. He thinks that even if God asked him such questions, he would let him have it. But what can he do here? There is unnecessary interference. It is like being served a good meal with grit in it! How can it taste good? Men and women should help each other. If the husband has worries, then the wife's main concern should be to find ways to reduce his worries. The husband should see that his wife is not placed in a difficult situation. The husband should realize how difficult the children can be. If things break in the house, men should not say even a word, but instead they complain, "Last time I bought the best cups and saucers and you broke them. You have destroyed everything." The wife will then think, "Did I break them deliberately? What can I do if they break? What can I do?" There is quarrelling even in such trivial matters. Why start quarrelling when there is nothing to gain? Where there is absolutely no reason to fight, why even start?

From the beginning, when I was young, I had made this division: the kitchen was hers and the business was mine. When I was young, I used to get very angry if any female member of our joint household asked me questions regarding the business accounts. This was not their business. People ask without any connection or cause. If you ask questions, there must be some connection or a reason to do so. If Hiraba were to ask me, "How much did you earn this year?" I would tell her that she did not have the right to ask me such a question because it was my personal matter. The reason for this is, if I let her ask me such questions today, and tomorrow I decide to give 500 rupees to someone, she would meddle in my business and complain about the money being gone. So do not interfere in people's personal matters.

[11] SUSPICION IS SELF DESTRUCTIVE

Most conflicts at home arise from doubts and suspicions. Suspicion gives rise to vibrations, which then ignite into flames. If a person were to become free of all suspicions, then these flames would extinguish. But if both the husband and wife start to become suspicious, then the flames would burn everything. One of them would have to become free of doubt. Quarrels between parents are the primary cause of emotional instability in children. In order to save their children, both parents must come to an understanding, bringing an end to all quarrelling. Who would be able to remove these suspicions? This *Gnan* of ours is such that it completely extinguishes your suspicions.

One man became suspicious of his wife. Would he be able to stop being suspicious of her? No! Such suspicion is a lifelong suspicion. Similarly the wife had suspicions about her husband, and that too, would not go away for a lifetime.

Questioner : What can we do, when suspicions arise against our wishes?

Dadashri : Possessiveness, a sense of ownership, "He is my husband," is the cause. There is nothing wrong in having a husband or even saying or referring to him as 'my husband,' but there must not be any attachment or possessiveness within.

Aim for two things in life, superficial trust and superficial suspicion. Do not venture too deeply into either. In the end, the person with doubts and suspicions will lose sanity and will have to be institutionalised. If ever a husband were to question the fidelity of his wife, she would call him an idiot and ask him to leave.

Men even become suspicious of their daughters when they go to school or away to college. Some will suspect their wives also. This is sheer betrayal. This era is filled with betrayal in the home; it is filled with nothing but deceit and betrayal. What possible happiness can he acquire? Whatever happiness people are striving for, they do so without any understanding of what true happiness is and furthermore they do everything in a state of stupor. People with pure intellect will not have any deceit or betrayal. Deceit and betrayal are to be found only in the foolish. In the current time cycle of *Kaliyug*, there is only the association of the foolish.

Even if others label a person as being immoral, you should consider him moral because in actuality he may not be immoral. If you call him immoral, then you face a very serious liability. If you call a virtuous woman, a prostitute, you are incurring a grave liability, the consequences of which you will have to endure for many lives to come. Therefore, do not say anything or comment about anyone's moral conduct. What if you are wrong? What is our own worth when we too make comments along with others? I have never made any such comments to or about anyone. I never interfere. Who would take on such a liability? You should never have any doubts about anyone's moral character. It is very dangerous. I will never allow suspicion. Why would I want to take on such a grave liability?

One man kept having doubts about his wife so I asked him the reason behind his suspicions. "Do you have doubts about her because you saw something? And was it not going on, even before you became aware of it?" I asked. People label the one who gets caught, a 'thief'. But even those who steal without getting caught are thieves. Here, only the ones who get caught are called thieves. You fools! Why are you calling him a thief? He was a simple man. He got caught because he was an amateur. The expert thieves never get caught.

Men who want peace of mind in regards to the conduct of their wives, should marry a woman who is unattractive, so that no one would want her. She herself would say, "Nobody wants to keep me. Only my husband will keep me, he is the only one who takes care of me." Then she would remain absolutely sincere to you. But if she is beautiful, then others undoubtedly will enjoy her. If she is beautiful, they will lust after her. Whenever someone marries a beautiful woman, I think of the predicament he is going to be in. If she is unattractive, only then there will be a safe side for him as far as his marriage is concerned.

When one has a beautiful wife, he will forget God, won't he? And if the husband is handsome, the wife will forget God. That is why the older generation had the saying, "Keep the farm *chopat* (flat) and a woman *kobaad* (unattractive, idiotic)."

What are these people like? They 'dine' wherever they see a 'hotel,' (the moment they see a woman, they will enjoy her). So there is no use in harbouring suspicions. Suspicions cause misery.

Some men are such that if the wife comes home a little late, they will become suspicious of her. Suspicion is something that you should absolutely shun. Nothing is going to happen outside the limits of your karmic account. When she comes home late, explain things to her but do not suspect her. Suspicion adds fuel to the fire. Alert her, but do not suspect her.

Those who harbour doubts lose their harmony and liberation.
So if you want to be liberated you should cast off all doubts.
Besides if you happen to see another man walking with his arm
around your wife, are you going to commit suicide?

So if you have any suspicions about anyone, do not
harbour them. Be cautious, but do not be suspicious. Suspicions
will kill you. Suspicions are such that they will not leave you
until you die. Regardless of what may happen to the other
person, *your* suspicion will surely kill you, because suspicion
will not leave you until you die. Suspicion makes a person live
like a corpse.

[12] FAULT OF DOMINANCE IN A HUSBAND

Questioner : There are some men who run away from
home because they get tired of their wives. What is that?

Dadashri : No, why should we become a runaway? We
are pure Souls, what is the need for us to become runaways?
We have to settle all matters with equanimity with our wives.

Questioner : I want to settle everything with equanimity,
but how do I go about doing that? Should I accept it in my
mind as a past account?

Dadashri : You cannot settle matters by just doing that
alone. Settling with equanimity means you have to make a
'phone call' to the other person's Soul. You must notify her
Soul. You must admit and accept your mistakes to that Soul.
You have to repent strongly and ask for forgiveness.

Questioner : Do I have to do *pratikraman* (Dada's
prescribed technique of confession, repentance, asking for
forgiveness, and vowing never to repeat the mistake) even if
someone insults me?

Dadashri : Do *pratikraman* only when they insult you,

not when they praise you. When you do *pratikraman*, feelings of hatred for that person will not arise at all. On the contrary, you will have a positive effect on him. In the first stage of your *pratikraman*, you will become aware of the fact that you do not have any abhorrence or negative feelings for him. Later on, the other person will also feel the positive effects of your *pratikraman*.

Questioner : Does it reach his Soul?

Dadashri : Yes, definitely. His Soul will nudge his *pudgal* (the physical body; the complex of thoughts, speech, and acts), "There is a phone call for you!" This *pratikraman* of ours is meant to destroy aggressive thoughts, speech, and acts.

Questioner : Do we have to do a lot of *pratikraman*?

Dadashri : If you want to build a house quickly, you will have to employ more builders. It is fine if you cannot do *pratikraman* for outsiders, but you must do a lot of *pratikraman* for those around you and those who are close to you. For the people in your home, you should keep the intention that, "These people are born close to me, they live together with me and some day they should take advantage of this wonderful science of liberation."

A man once came to me and said, "Dada I am married now, but I do not like my wife." I asked him his reason, and he told me he did not like her because she walked with a limp. So I asked him "Does your wife like you?" He replied, "Dada, I am a likeable person! I am handsome, educated, I earn good money, and I do not have any deformities." I told him, "Then the fault is yours. What kind of a mistake did you make to deserve a limping wife like her and what good karma did she have to get a great husband like you? Listen here, it is all your own doing that is coming back to you. So then why are you looking at faults in her? Suffer the fruits of your past mistakes with equanimity and do not make any new mistakes." The man understood this and his life, which was on the verge of ruins, became harmonious.

[13] ALL HUSBANDS ! ACT ACCORDING TO DADA'S VISION

Questioner : What should I do when my wife says she doesn't want my parents to live with us, or that I am not to call them?

Dadashri : Work through it by making her understand. Do it through a democratically. Call her parents and take really good care of them.

Questioner : If I have to choose between my parents and my wife, whom should I listen to first?

Dadashri : Improve your relationship with your wife to the extent that she herself will tell you to take care of your parents. Why are you behaving this way? You should say a few negative things about your parents to your wife, to make her feel that you are in her favour. But what do men say instead? "No one has a mother like mine. You better not say anything to her." Then if your wife gets upset, you should tell her, "Mother's nature has become that way. Do not mind her. Forgive her." The Indian mind has a propensity towards changing in the wrong direction.

Do you know there are some men who make their wives their Guru?

Questioner : Yes, I do.

Dadashri : It is not advisable to make your wife your guru; if you do you will put your parents and all your family members in difficulty, including yourself. There will be times when you will have to play her also, but you will not be able to do that if you make her your boss. This does not happen to those who come to me. With my *Gnan* their life together becomes filled with harmony. All subtle, internal violence disappears. All they think about is how to make other people happy.

You have to be careful and compromising, especially with a new wife. If everything is new, then you have to help her adjust. If the wife sulks on the first day and you get upset, nothing good will come about. If she sulks, pacify her and tell her the two of you are one. Try to appease her in this manner. What happens if you both start shouting? Shouldn't you know how to deal with your wife?

Questioner : Some ladies get tired of the routine house chores. When you ask them to do something, they come up with all kinds of excuses, such as "I am tired, my head hurts, my back hurts."

Dadashri : Start in the morning by saying her, "My dear you are tired today. Why don't you take a break and rest?" This will energize her. She will reply, "No you be quiet and sit down, I will take care of it." We should be masters in the art convincing others to do work.

Questioner : When we are driving, she tells me how to drive, where to take a turn, when to slow down, and when to apply the brakes. She is always nagging, "Drive this way, and drive that way."

Dadashri : So leave the driving to her, then there will be no hassle.

Questioner : Then she'll say she does not have the courage to drive.

Dadashri : Then ask her why she interferes with your driving. Ask her if your driving is hurting her in any way. Tell her that the only reason she gets away with her criticisms is because you are her husband. Ask her if she would criticize the chauffer the same way. She knows that if she did, he would tell her to be quiet or get out, putting her in a predicament.

Questioner : If we do not take the wife's side, there will be a fight.

Dadashri : Correct, and there is nothing wrong in doing so. If you take her side, only then will you have a peaceful night. Otherwise how would you be able to sleep? In these kinds of situations, you should not use your intellect as a lawyer.

Questioner : We should not side with the neighbours when they fight with our wives, should we?

Dadashri : No, in all disputes, you should always take the side of your wife, not the neighbours, even if your wife is at fault. Take care of the people in your own home first. Even if your wife is guilty, you should defend her. There you do not need to look for justice and accuse her of wrongdoing. You have to eat and sleep here only. You should plead the case in support of your own family.

Questioner : How can we tell whether the other party has been satisfied? The other party may be satisfied but what if there is harm in it for them?

Dadashri : That is not your look out. If there is harm in it for them, it is their lookout. You should take into consideration what is good or bad for others, but do you really have the ability to do so? You are not able to see what is good or bad for your own self, so why are you looking for the good or the bad for others? Each individual looks for what is in his own best interest according to his own capacity. There should not be any conflict in trying to do good for the other person.

Questioner : When we make an effort to ending a conflict with someone and we know that the result is not going to be satisfactory, what should we do?

Dadashri : The end result may be anything, but all you have to do is make a decision to put an end to it. Decide to settle with equanimity. Then do not be concerned with whether there is closure or not. It will happen, if not today then some day. If it (your karmic account) is sticky, it may take two or three or five years. Karmic accounts with your wife, children, and parents are very sticky and complex, and therefore, closure with them will take longer. These relatives are always with us. Here settlement will take time, but if you have made the decision that you do want to settle with equanimity, then one day it will settle. It will come to an end.

[14] UNWIND THE STRINGS OF BONDAGE WITH YOUR WIFE IN THIS MANNER

One day a man came to me crying, so I asked him what was wrong. He told me, "My young wife died recently and I cannot stop thinking about her. I have two young children." I then asked how long they had been married. "Exactly twelve years today," he replied. So then I asked him if he would have had feelings for her had he met her on a bus twelve and a half years ago, to which he replied, "No."

Don't they sit the bride and the groom under the *chori* (a canopy under which the Hindu marriage ceremony is conducted) during the wedding ceremony? As he sits in the *chori*, he looks at the woman across from him, and says to himself, "Yes, this is my wife." When he tells himself this, he winds the first knot of, "My wife." Countless twists of, "My wife, my wife, my wife," begin to accumulate within him. From the moment he sat down under the *chori*, he kept winding the knots of 'my wife' in this manner, and that winding continues till this moment, so just imagine how many knots he has wound. How is he going to unwind these knots? These are the knots of *mamta* (attachment).

I told him that from that moment on, he would have to keep reciting, "Not mine, not mine, not mine." He would have to keep telling himself, "This woman is not mine, she is not mine." This way all the knots he had tied, would unravel. If you have tied fifty thousand knots by saying "Mine, mine, mine," then by saying "Not mine, not mine, not mine," fifty thousand times over, you will free yourself from your attachment. What is this meaningless obsession?

So then what did he do? For three days, he kept saying, "She is not mine, she is not mine, she is not mine," and by doing he was able to stop crying. His grief vanished. All these are merely knots that we have entwined and it is because of these knots that we suffer. All such suffering is false. Do you understand what I am saying? Now who is going to show you such a simple, straightforward way?

All day long you should continue doing *pratikraman* for your husband. When you do this, six months worth of ill feelings will be destroyed in just one day. Even if you do it for half a day, at least three months will be cleared. Did you have any attachment with your husband before you got married? No. So when did this attachment start? It was decided when the two of you sat across from each other under the wedding canopy and you thought to yourself, "This is my husband. He is a little plump and dark-skinned." He too, decided, "This is my wife." From that moment onwards these knots of, "My, my," started. This film has been going on for fifteen years, and it will only unwind, if you say, "He is not mine, he is not mine." Only then, this false attachment will end. These opinions have arisen from the time of your marriage. Prejudices of, "He's like this. He's like that," have taken hold. Were they ever there before? Now you have to decide, "No matter what he is like, he is the only one for me." You yourself had selected him. Is it appropriate for you to ask for a different husband now?

[15] RECOGNITION OF THE HIGHEST LOVE

Someone may ask, "Isn't a woman's love worth appreciating?" Then I would explain to him that love, which increases or decreases, is not true love at all. Her love will increase when you buy her a pair of diamond earrings, but will then decrease if you refuse to buy her a diamond ring. This is not love.

Questioner : So in the absence of increase or decrease, what is the nature of real love?

Dadashri : Real love does not increase or decrease. In all events and situations, real love remains constant. Here, your love will remain as long as they are doing your work, and it will break when they refuse to do you work. How can you call this love? You will find pure love, where there are no selfish motives. And where will you find no selfishness? There is no selfishness where there are no feelings of 'mine' or 'yours'. Where there is *Gnan* (knowledge of the Real Self), there are no feelings of 'mine' or 'yours'! There is always 'mine' and 'yours,' where there is no *Gnan*.

All of these beliefs are wrong. "I am Chandubhai," is a wrong belief. Then when we go to his house, we ask, "Who is this?" and he will reply, "Did you not recognize me? I am this woman's *dhani* (husband; owner)." All these are wrong beliefs. Why do you want to be her owner (husband)? What is wrong in saying that she is your companion?

Questioner : Dada, you just used a very modern word.

Dadashri : What then? Only then will these arguments stop. When two companions live in one room, they share all the chores. That is how companionship is maintained.

Questioner : Is there any infatuation or fascination in companionship?

Dadashri : There is attachment in it, but that attachment is not like a fire. You need to recognize the force and the power behind words. The words, 'husband' and 'wife' are filled with intense infatuation and attachment, but that attachment becomes weaker when you use the word 'companion'.

One man had lost his wife twenty years ago. At that time, a young boy came to me and asked me, "Shall I make this man cry?" I asked him, "How are you going to do that? He would not cry at this age." The young man replied, "Just wait and see how sensitive he is." Then he started to talk to the man, "Uncle, what a lady your wife was, what a great personality she had." When he said this, the old man started to cry. What a foolish man, he still cries about his wife at the age of sixty. How foolish are these people? People also cry at the movies, don't they? If someone dies in a movie, the people in the audience start crying.

Questioner : So why can't we get rid of this sense of attachment?

Dadashri : You cannot get rid of it. That which you have created by saying, "Mine, mine," can only be undone by saying, "Not mine, not mine." All the knots you have created will have to be unwound. All this is sheer attachment. There is nothing real in it; there is no life in it. Every person here is nothing but wound up toys.

Wherever there is attachment, there is bound to be accusations. That is the nature of attachment. When people accuse each other of doing certain things or behaving a certain way is due to attachment. Do people not say such things? They say such things because of attachment.

Girls today choose their husbands after close scrutiny, but later get angry with them. Do they not quarrel with their husbands? So then you cannot call that love at all, can you? Love should be unwavering. Whenever you see it, it is the same love. That is where you will find consolation. Here you may have love for her but if the next day she is shouts, then you will think to yourself, "To hell with this love. Dump it in the sewer!" What good is such a love, when she walks around sulking all the time? What do you think?

Human nature is such that wherever there is excessive love, (love with attachment and expectations; conditional love), therein there exists an undercurrent of abhorrence and repulsion.

On the way to the movies, a couple starts off in a state of mutual excitement and infatuation. On their way back home, the repulsion starts, they get into a fight. He tells her, 'you have not sense' and she responds, 'and what wisdom do you have?' In this manner they both come home talking and arguing. He looks for sense and she is looking for wisdom.

One can only improve with real love. All these people have felt my love and have improved. Love is my real nature, and hence there is no scope for discord. Whenever I say things to people, I speak with nothing but love and that is why nothing spoils. If I were to speak with even a hint of dislike, it would ruin everything.

Questioner : Please explain the difference between real love and love associated with attachment.

Dadashri : The love that goes beyond its natural boundary is love of attachment and attraction. What the world calls love is love of this kind; it is a state of temporary attraction that is subject to repulsion.

This attraction and so-called 'love' is like the attraction between a magnet and a needle. There is no such thing as love in it. The inner force that draws man and woman together is similar to the attraction between a needle and a magnet. Not being aware of this phenomenon, he thinks it is love that is pulling him. Real love exists in the heart of a *Gnani*, the Awakened One.

Pure Love is The Absolute Self. There is no other definition of the Absolute Self. That is the only location where final peace and harmony exists. That is the only place where the heart will rest. The heart will be soothed in two ways, through a woman, and through a *Gnani*. The woman will make you slip into the worldly life. The *Gnani* will free you from the worldly life, liberating you forever.

Love that is free from anger, pride, greed, and attachment, love that is beyond the sexual genders, love that remains constant, love that neither decreases nor increases, is called 'pure love'. This is the love of the *Gnani*. This is where the heart rests.

I am the embodiment of pure love. If you become intoxicated with this love, you will forget the world. Find this love, feel its intoxication, and your world will run smoothly and harmoniously.

[16] MARRIAGE IS A PROMISSARY NOTE "PROMISE TO PAY"

In 1943, Hiraba lost one of her eyes to glaucoma. In the process of trying to correct this condition, her eye was damaged even more.

People started thinking, "Now we have a new groom. Let's get him married again." At that time there were many prospective brides. The attitude of the parents at the time was that it did not matter what the groom was like, their daughters must get married. In the year 1944, I was thirty-six years old. A Patel from Bhadran, (Dada's town), approached me one day in regards to his wife's brother had a daughter. When I asked him why he had come to me he said, "You have just had a mishap. First of all, Hiraba has lost her eye and on top of that you do not have any children." I told him, "I don't have any children but neither do I have any estate in terms of wealth. All I have is a small piece of land and a roof over my head" I had no estate for posterity. But why are you asking me all this? The day I married Hiraba, I had made a promise to her. So what if she has lost her eye, what can be done now? Even if she lost both her eyes, I would hold her hand and guide her."

Questioner : We both came to know each other better after we got married and now we feel that we made an error of judgment in choosing each other. We are incompatible with each other. What should we do to become compatible with each other so that we can be happy?

Dadashri : Everything you have said so far is false. First you said that you got to know each other better after marriage, however this is not true. You have not understood anything. If you understood each other, there would be no problems.

I stopped all disputes in my marriage after getting rid of my interfering intellect. Only then was I able to really know my wife. When did I come to understand Hiraba? When I was sixty years old. I got married at the age of fifteen, so for forty-five years I observed closely and only then, did I come to understand what she was like.

Questioner : So you acquired the understanding after you attained *Gnan*?

Dadashri : Yes! I came to understand her after I attained *Gnan*. Otherwise one will not be able to understand. A person does not have the capacity to understand his wife. A man is not able to understand what he himself is all about, let alone his wife! Therefore, this sentence you uttered, "We understand each other," has no meaning. Neither of you have made a mistake in choosing each other.

Questioner : Explain to me how I should come to understand. How can one slowly and subtly understand her with love? How can a husband do that for his wife? Explain this.

Dadashri : When can you understand? When you make her your equal. Next, give her space. You only enjoy a game of checkers when both sides have equal rights in taking turns. However, in marriage, where do men give equal rights? I give equal rights.

Questioner : How do you do this? How can this be done practically?

Dadashri : Even in your mind, you should not regard her as a separate entity, nor should she feel separate from you. Even when her speech is inappropriate, you should treat her as an equal; in this manner you will not bring any pressure on her.

So try to recognize the other person's *prakruti*. Then try to find some other ways that can help you. Don't I try different methods to get people to do things? Don't people do as I tell them? They do and it is not because I have the skills, it is because I use different methods. They do not feel that they are under any pressure.

Even if you do not like staying at home, you have to say to her, "I do not like being away from you." Only then will you be able attain liberation. Now that you have met Dada, you will definitely attain liberation.

Questioner : Do you say that to Hiraba?

Dadashri : Yes, I say that to Hiraba, even now.

Even at my age I say to Hiraba, "I do not like it when I am away from you." Now she probably would be thinking to herself, "I like it, why does he not like it?" When you speak in this manner, then your home life will be full of harmony. Pour some cream on it, enrich your life with your wife, otherwise it will be too dry. Pour in some beautiful feelings. Here she (Hiraba) is sitting, as I speak. When she asks me if she is in my thoughts, I tell her, "Yes, very much. All other people come to my mind, so why would you And really, she is in my thoughts.

Our life is ideal. Hiraba will even tell me to come home early.

When can one be said to have fulfilled the role of a husband? It is when the wife develops a constant reverence for him. What should a husband be like? He should never let any difficulties befall upon his wife or his children. And what should the wife be like? Such, that she never causes problems for him. She should constantly live with this awareness.

[17] QUARRELS WITH WIFE

When husband and wife are fighting verbally, it is generally superficial. They do not harbour any vengeance from within. If you were to interfere and come in between, they will get their work done but eventually they will always stick together. Fights that do not result in separation are merely parrot talks and parrot fights. I would instantly recognize that these two are in a parrot fight and they should not be taken seriously.

If you scold your wife, servant, or children for just one hour, then in your next life they will come to you as your wife or mother-in-law and harass you for the rest of your life. Justice is always there. You cannot avoid this suffering. If you create misery for anyone, you will get the same dose back. An hour's worth of misery given to others will result in a lifetime of pain for you. Then you will complain, "My wife is no good, she nags me." The wife may wonder herself why she is the cause of your misery. She suffers too. But there is no way out. Then if I were to ask this man, "Did you chose her to be your wife or did she chose you to be her husband?" he would say that he chose her. So why blame her? It is not her fault if later on, you find her unsuitable. Where can she go?

Questioner : Can things be resolved if we stop talking in order to bring the matter to close?

Dadashri : No, nothing will get resolved. If you meet that person, you should ask him how he is doing. But if he starts acting up a little and becomes loud and aggressive, you should maintain your calmness and solve the matter with equanimity. Sooner or later, you will have to deal with it. If you stop talking to him, does that mean things have been resolved? It's just the opposite. It is because the problem has not been solved that people stop talking to each other. When people stop talking, it means there is a burden, a burden of not being able to resolve the problem. You should immediately say, "Tell me if I have made a mistake. I make a lot of mistakes. You are very educated and clever, therefore you don't make too many mistakes, but I am less educated so I make a lot of mistakes!" You have to talk to him in this manner so that he will be happy and come around.

Questioner : What should I do if when I say this to him, he still does not come around?

Dadashri : If he does not soften up, then what can you do? You just do your best and free yourself from your side. What other solution is there? One day he will soften up. If you try to soften him by telling him off, it will not work. Today he may appear to have softened, but he will make a note in his mind and then one day when you are soft, he will rehash everything. This world is full of vengeance. It is the law of nature that every living being will harbor some vengeance. They will retain the atoms of vengeance. You should always try to solve all conflicts.

Questioner : So then should we not say anything at all?

Dadashri : Yes you should, but only if the other person accepts it whole-heartedly. Otherwise what is the point of barking like a dog? Whatever you say, should be acceptable to the other person.

Questioner : But what am I to do if he is lying?

Dadashri : Whether he lies or not, it is not your look out. Whether he speaks the truth or lies, it is his responsibility.

Questioner : If we do not know how to say it, then should we just keep quiet?

Dadashri : Remain silent and see what happens. If you are watching a movie, and a child falls in that movie, what do you do? Everyone has the right to say something but only to the point where it will not create any friction and hostility. It is foolish to speak when doing so exacerbates the problem.

When your words are filled with real love, then even if you scold them, they will not be hurt.

Questioner : Yes, that is of importance.

Dadashri : There is nothing wrong in telling people off when you are free from the weakness of attachment and abhorrence. It is this weakness that is the problem.

Questioner : What should we do when we don't want to start any fights or arguments at all, but others in the house start them daily?

Dadashri : You should become 'fight-proof'. If you become 'fight-proof' then will you be able to live in this world peacefully. I will make you 'fight-proof.' You should become so fight-proof that even the person that comes to fight with you gets tired and gives up. No one in this world can depress you. You have to become that way. If you become fight-proof, then there are no problems. If others want to fight or swear at you, even then there will be no objection or reaction. No one will call you indifferent for being that way. On the contrary, your internal awareness of *Gnan* (*jagruti*) will increase.

Whatever disputes you created in the past life, created vengeance, and today it dissipates in the form of a dispute or disagreement. A seed of revenge is planted at the time of arguments, and this seed will grow in the next life.

Questioner : So how can you avoid sowing such seeds?

Dadashri : Slowly and steadily, if you keep on settling your problems with equanimity you can prevent new seeds from being sowed. If the causal karma was very heavy, you will have to be patient because it will take time to solve. You have to do a lot of *pratikraman*. Nobody will take anything away from you. You have a shirt on your back and you get two meals a day, what more do you need? They (your children) may lock you up in your room before they go out, but at least you still get two meals a day, so just rest and go to sleep quietly. They lock you up because such were the seeds of vengeance. It is nothing but vengeance, and what is more, it was created in ignorance. All consequences of acts done in ignorance will have to be endured, without fail.

Now in order to let go of all the vengeance, come to me and take this *Gnan* (knowledge) of Self-realization. All vengeance will be dissolved. You have to let go of all the vengeance and negative feelings in this very lifetime. I will show you the way.

When the mosquitoes or the bedbugs bite, those bites are much better than the bites from a husband or wife. Dealing with all that, is very tough. Do husband and wife not bite eachother?

Questioner : Yes, they do.

Dadashri : So that biting needs to stop. The mosquitoes will bite and leave when their stomachs are full. But the wife is constantly biting her husband. One man told me, "My wife bites me like a snake." You fool! Then why did you marry this snake? You have to be a snake in order to marry one!

If you had nothing to do with your wife after you quarrel with her, then it would be a different matter, but you still have to speak to her again, so the quarrelling in between is wrong. I am always aware of the fact that after an hour or so we will have to speak to each other again, therefore I never argue. It would be a different matter altogether if your opinion were never to change, or you were never to be with her again. Only then your quarrelling would be acceptable, but here you will have to sit and dine together the very next day. So does that mean that all your quarrelling was just a drama? What happened to the scene you created yesterday? Should you not think about that?

The husband should be the first to repent. The husband

should be open-minded. The wife should not be the first to ask for forgiveness. Men, by nature, are more forgiving. Do you understand what I am saying?

Questioner : He is pleased since you said that husbands have a more forgiving nature.

Dadashri : No, men really do have an open and forgiving mind; they have a very open mind and women are more natural and spontaneous in their actions. This means that if it comes to their mind from within to ask for forgiveness, they will. If it does not arise in their mind, they will not repent. But if you, as a husband, take the initiative and ask for forgiveness, then she too will do so immediately. You will not remain completely dependant upon your unfolding karma; you are dependant upon your *jagruti* (awareness), but she is dependent upon her unfolding karma. Women are spontaneous and natural. Such natural spontaneity is not a trait in men. If indeed you were to acquire that trait, you would be very happy.

Questioner : Ego is wrong, that is what we are told and we even listen. We hear it over and over again. All scriptures and religious teachers preach this too. Despite this, why does this ego not go?

Dadashri : When will ego leave? When you accept it is wrong, only then will it leave. If you fight with your wife, then you should understand that your ego is wrong. Therefore everyday through that very ego, you should ask for her forgiveness, from within. Then the ego will go away. You will have to find a solution, will you not?

I am showing you this straightforward path. Besides you do not clash with your wife on a daily basis, do you? It only happens as your karmas unfold, and for that you just need to adjust accordingly. After an altercation with your wife, take her out to dinner and make her happy. From now on, the sulking should not linger and there should be no internal grudges against each other.

So now that you have this *Gnan*, that problem will not remain. If you have *Gnan*, then you will see the Real (Soul) in your wife, first thing in the morning. You will have to see the God in your wife, will you not? If you can see Dada in your wife, then salvation is yours. When you look at your wife, can you see Dada? You can see pure Soul. Then salvation is yours.

So adjust in any way you can. Time will pass and your accounts will be cleared. You will have to honour your debts of karma from your past life. For some debts it may take twenty-five years, some, fifteen years, and others, thirty years. You don't have a choice. Even if you don't like it, you will have to stay within the same room. On one side, will be her bed and on the other side will be your bed. Even if you turn around and face the other direction, both of you will only have thoughts of each other. There is no way out. The whole world is like this.

It is not just that you don't like her, she doesn't like you either. So this world is not such that you can extract any real enjoyment out of it.

Don't see laws, please settle. Settle any conflict with equanimity. Where do we have the time to tell the other person, "Do it this way, settle it this way,"? Even if the other person has made a hundred mistakes, you have to take it as your own fault and just move on. There is no time to lose the fight against the laws of the world, even if you are right. In this day and age, one cannot afford to look at the law. This is a very serious matter. You are at the end of your rope of infinite lives. Such opportunity will not come again.

Questioner : Sometimes there is a major fight in the home. What should we do?

Dadashri : A wise man would refuse to quarrel even if someone gave him a million rupees and yet here, people quarrel without getting paid. If that is not foolishness, what is it? Lord Mahavir had to walk sixty miles to estranged areas in order to fulfil his karmas at the hands of primitive people. But today you fortunate people do not have to venture out of your homes to settle your karmas. How fortunate you are! All this (quarrelling) is very beneficial for settling your karmas, providing you know how to conduct yourself.

Give advice or your opinions, only if someone in the household asks. The Lord has said that to give advice without being asked is egotistical. A husband asks his wife where to stack the water glasses and she tells him. But instead he tells her that is not a good place to store the glasses and that she has no sense and starts an argument. She replies, "I don't have any sense and that is why I told you to put them there. Now you use your own sense and put them wherever you want." How can you solve these kinds of quarrels? These are all merely clashes of circumstances. These tops (Dada calls all human beings 'tops'; we are all tops spinning in this life and our spinning is dictated by our past karma as they come to fruition) clash as they eat or as they wake up. These tops then become bruised and even bleed. This is all mental bleeding. Bleeding from a physical wound is preferable because you can stop it with a bandage, but you cannot put any dressing on these mental injuries.

You cannot attain *moksh* if you insult anyone in your family or outside. Insults associated with abhorrence are very dangerous. It will surely impede your liberation. There are varying degrees of insults. One can have mild internal repulsion and internal hate, which is not apparent to others. Then there are overt, intense insults with abhorrence, which cause severe mental wounds in the person insulted, and for that one will have to endure a lot of misery in the next life.

One lady told me she felt as if I was her father from her past life. She was very nice and very cultured. I asked her how she got along with her husband. She told me that he does not say anything. He is always calm and composed. I asked her surely some days they must have some disagreements. She said no but sometimes he would make a cynical comment. I understood. So I asked her what she would do when he made sarcastic comments, I asked if she would strike back at him. She replied, "No, I tell him that we are together due to the unfolding of our karmas. I am separate and you are separate. So why are you doing this? Why do have to make sarcastic comments and what is all this about? No one is at fault here. It is the fault of the unfolding of the karmas. So instead of making sarcastic comments, why don't you settle your karmas with equanimity? Why should we clash?" I have seen many women, but this is the only woman I have seen with such an elevated understanding.

My inherent qualities are that of a *kshatriya* (warrior, kingly class). Instilled within me, I have the ability to protect those under me and I do not fear taking on my superiors. This is the main quality of a *kshatriya*. I always protect my wife and servants who depend on me, even when they are at fault. I would not say anything to the poor man, but if it were someone above me, I would fight with him. The world generally harasses its subordinates. You idiot! Are you a woman? A woman would treat a subordinate in this manner. What do you think of this?

You get married; bring her home, and then you keep scolding her. What is this comparable to? It is like tying a cow to a pole and flogging her. What would happen if you were to tie her to a pole and kept hitting her? If you hit her from one side, the poor thing will go to the other side. Where will she go if she is tied up? The 'societal pole' is such that she cannot escape. If you hit someone who is tied down, you create tremendous misery for yourself in your life to come. What if she were not tied down and then you were to hit her? That is different and it would not be as serious. If she were not tied down, then she would be able to escape. But here she has the pressure of the society and therefore she cannot go anywhere. Otherwise she would be long gone. Try to hit her after getting a divorce. What would happen?

A real husband is one who never has any discord with his wife. Just as you would not let anything come between you and your friend, in the same manner you should do the same when dealing with her also. If you do not look out for your friend, your friendship will end. Friendship means friendship. You have to challenge her by saying, "If you break this friendship of ours, then you will be at fault. Let us live in harmony as friends."

There is so much sincerity in a friendship that the friend would say, "I have a wonderful friend. He would never have a single negative thought about me." In that same manner you cannot think badly of her either. Is she not considered more than a friend?

[18] SHE WILL AVENGE YOU WITH A SLEDGE HAMMER

Now if you both were to have an argument one night, she would have a *tanto* (prolonged inner anger and turmoil). The next morning, when serving you your tea, she would deliberately slam the cup down on the table. This would tell you that she has not quite recovered from the fight the night before. That verily is the link between the argument the night before and her current state of continued sulking.

Why does she continue sulking? It is because she wants

you under her thumb (wrapped around her finger). If you get angry, she will know that you have become weak, but if you don't get angry, then she will try harder.

If, despite her continued arguing, the husband does not get angry, then she will go into the kitchen and throw a few utensils around to make noise... Bang...bang!! When he hears the noise he will get upset, but if he does not, then at this point, she will pinch their little toddler and make him cry. Then he will get angry! "You are after our son now? Why are you bringing our son in the middle of this?" Then she will be satisfied, "Ah ha! Now he is defeated!"

Men forget events, whereas women will hold on to them their entire lives. Men are naive, open-minded, and forgiving. They will forget. Women on the other hand will keep reminding you of what you said the day of the fight. Heavens! Even after twenty years, her memory is so fresh. Your son is now twenty years old, old enough to get married, yet she continues to hang on to that incident. Everything except for her memory will rot! When you hurt a woman, she will keep it in a special place in her heart, so never hurt her. You must be very cautious in this matter.

Whenever you hurt a woman through your words, you are inviting a liability for your future. She will tolerate you for the time being because you are stronger than her, but later when you are weak and all your joints are creaking, she will take her revenge, so watch out. I have witnessed this many times over. That is why I advise men not to fight. "You fools! Don't fight with your wives. Do not bind any vengeance with your wives. Otherwise you will create grave difficulties."

By their true nature, our women are like goddesses. The worldly interactions defile their true nature and they become dangerous. She has the to go into an explosive rage if instigated or hurt excessively. Hence, the saying, "It is easy to play with and please a woman, but when she gets angry, she is a terror." When she gets angry she is like a lioness. We men should not take things that far, we should know our limits. If you keep harassing the poor woman, where will she go? That is why she gets angry. Her response of anger varies in intensity, from mild to extreme.

When a woman is in an explosive rage, your intellect will not help you. Your intellect will not be able to control her, so speak to her in a manner that will not aggravate her. Keep real love in your eyes. If at any time she says the wrong things, remember that she is a woman and let it go. Have complete love in one eye and in the other, maintain a little sternness. You should live in this manner. Use the appropriate approach. You cannot be totally strict all day long. In one eye you maintain strictness and with the other eye view her as a goddess. Do you understand?

Questioner : How can you be strict in one eye and view her as a goddess in the other at the same time?

Dadashri : A man is capable of all that. When I was about thirty years old, whenever I came home, Hiraba would be visiting with other ladies. Not just Hiraba, but the other ladies too, would see sternness as well as reverence in my eyes. The ladies would be sitting with their faces covered by the veil of their *saris*, but the moment I entered the house, they would stiffen up. Hiraba too, would be fearful even before I entered the home. The minute she heard my footsteps, fear overcame her. Maintain strictness in one eye and love in the other. A woman cannot live without this control and love from a man. That is why Hiraba used to say, "Goodness, just look at what Dada is like!"

Questioner : Very hot tempered.

Dadashri : Very hot-tempered; I used to maintain this, always. But you don't have to scare her unnecessarily. As soon as I entered, everything became quiet. Everything cools down, the instant my footsteps are heard.

Why the strictness? It is to prevent her from falling in life. That is why you should have the look of control in one eye and love in the other.

I am often accused of siding with the women. I am telling you to praise your wife, but that does not mean you need to do her *aarti* (devotional ritual) in the morning. If you do that, then she will wear and tear you down. What do I mean by this? I tell you to have sternness in one eye and love in the other eye, but don't put her on a pedestal. She does not have those qualities. Praise her in your mind.

Questioner : You have spoken about men, but what should women do? What should women maintain in their eyes?

Dadashri : For a woman, regardless of what her husband is like, she has to accept him as her own account. It is not coincidental that one acquires a husband. No matter what your husband is like, your efforts should be put into becoming a devoted wife. If you are not able to do this, then ask for his forgiveness. This should be your aim. You should be focused on how you can progress further in your partnership with your husband. How will you attain a higher level; how you will both attain *moksha*?

So tell your wife, "*You* can fight with me as much as you want, but Dada has told me not to fight. Dada has given me this command, so I am going to sit here and you can say whatever you want to say."

Questioner : Then she will remain quiet.

Dadashri : She will become silent when you bring up Dada's name; there is no other weapon. Use this weapon freely.

A lady once said to me, "When I got married, my husband was very dominant." I asked, "How is he now?" She proceeded, "Dada, you know all about women's behaviour, so why are you making me say it? When he wants some happiness from me, I tell him to address me as 'master'. In this way I make him do what I want. What fault is it of mine? Before he used to make me call him 'master', and now I make him say it."

When a powerful officer came home after a frustrating day at work, his wife said, "You are an hour and half late! Where have you been?" Just look at this, a man with lion-like qualities being scolded, a man whom the whole state of Gujarat fears, being scolded like a child. Nobody dare cross him, and yet his own wife did not respect him and not only that, she even reprimanded him. So one day I told her, "What if this husband of yours were to leave you alone and go out of town for a fortnight or so?" She said she would be scared. Now what is she scared of? So she tells me, "When I hear a noise in the other room, I think that there may be is a ghost there." I told her, "You get scared even if a mouse knocks something over, but if your husband were in the house you would not feel scared. You keep scolding and nagging at him, to the point where he feels like nothing. You reduce this lion of a husband of yours to nothing but a sheep!"

One man bought a mare for three thousand rupees. Everyday he used to sit on the mare. One day his twenty-four year old son rode the mare to the local pond. He teased the horse a little. Is a three thousand rupee mare supposed to be teased? Rather than being teased or instigated, she must be allowed to walk in her own style and at her own pace. When the son teased her, she pounced and as she did that, the young man fell to the ground. So what did he say when he got home? "Sell this horse, the horse is bad!" He is the one who does not know how to sit on the horse and he is blaming the horse! The definition of a dominant husband is the one who blames and belittles the horse because he does not know how to sit on her or ride her. Should you not know how to treat your wife?

If a husband opposes his wife just once, he loses his dignity. The wife will lose respect for him. If your household is running smoothly, the children are doing well in school, and you have no other bothers and yet you scold your wife and find faults with her, then your wife will lose respect for you. She will know that you have no substance.

You do not know how to deal with the ladies. If you, as a shopkeeper, do not know how to deal with your customers, they will not come to you. Don't people say, "Hire a good salesman."? If the salesman is good, handsome, and clever, then people would be willing to pay more. In the same manner, you should know how to conduct your dealings with your wife.

It is because there is a presence of a woman, that this world has warmth and joy in it. Otherwise in your household you would be worse than a hermit. The cleaning and sweeping would not be done in the morning. There would be no signs of tea, or breakfast. It is only upon the instructions of the wife, that one takes a timely bath. It is because of her that there is a glow and warmth in the home; and her joy is because of him.

Women have a tremendous tolerance for pain and suffering. Even when times are very difficult and there is grave suffering, she will tell her husband, "Don't be afraid, just go to sleep, why are you making yourself unhappy?" She will pacify him.

A woman by nature is spontaneous and natural. When the husband incurs a loss of five hundred thousand dollars or so, he will worry the whole day long about it. If his business is running at a loss, he will not eat properly. A woman on the other hand, will tell him to stop worrying unnecessarily. She will tell him to eat properly. She is also a fifty percent partner in the business. Why does she not worry? It is because she is *sahaj* (spontaneous and natural). When you live with *sahaj* people, then you will survive, otherwise you will not. If on the other hand, two men were to live together, they would not find any meaningful comfort from being with each other. The woman is *sahaj*, and it is because of her presence, that there is joy in the home.

A woman is a Goddess of strength. If a man understands this, his life's work is done. The woman is not at fault; the fault lies in man's wrong understanding. Women are Goddesses. Do not try to make them any lesser. You should say she is a Goddess. You may even call her, '*Devi*' (Goddess). In northern India, in many places they address their women as 'Devi'. Even nowadays, they say, "Shardadevi has come," or "Manidevi has come." Don't they say this in certain places?

If four men were to live together, one of them would cook, and the others would do something else. Even if the chores were divided, that household would be useless and no fun to live in. If one man and one woman were to live in a home, that home would be beautiful. Women really know how to make things beautiful.

Questioner : Don't keep siding with just the women, Dada!

Dadashri : I am not siding with the women, I am really siding with the men, but women think I am siding with them. In reality, I am siding with the men, because you men are the head of the family. She is not the owner of the family, you are the owner. In Bombay people asked me why I side with women as opposed to men. I replied, "Lord Mahavir was born to a woman, who are you men going to give birth to?" You people are making a big issue for no reason.

Questioner : Still, you are partial towards the women. This is what we believe.

Dadashri : Yes. People have accused me of that, but at the same time I raise men up so high, that even women start to respect them. I arrange things in such a way. If you look at it, on the surface, it appears that I am siding with the women, but from within I root for the men. Therefore, there has to be ways to arrange things. Both parties need to be satisfied.

I get along very well with women as well as men. I neither side with men, nor do I side with women. Both have to be equally responsible. People in the past have made women inferior. Women are helpful. If the woman were not there, how would your household run?

[19] COMPLAINTS FROM THE WIFE

If you complain you will become a complainer. If anyone comes to me complaining about someone, I consider him to be a guilty party. Why has an occasion arisen for him to complain? Most complainers are usually the perpetrators. Being the wrongdoer himself, he comes to complain. If you complain, you will become the complainer and the other person will be the accused. In his eyes you become the accuser. So never make a complaint against anyone.

If the other person is multiplying the conflict by complaints and discord, you should use division and try to achieve peace by settling the matter with equanimity. To spend time thinking about why a person caused you hurt is a grave mistake. If you bump into a wall, why do you not get angry with the wall? Everyone that comes to collide with you is like the wall or a tree. When a cow steps on your foot, do you get angry and start fighting with it? The same should be with people also. How does the *Gnani Purush* forgive everyone? He knows that all the people are like the wall and the tree. They do not understand, and the one who *does* have the understanding will not need to be told. Those who have the understanding will immediately start their *pratikraman*.

What do you do when your husband insults you? Do you start a claim against him?

Questioner : No, that is not right.

Dadashri : Then what do you do? Do you go to bed saying, "I bless you," or do you keep cursing him in your mind? Generally there is a lot of hostility from within.

If a beautiful *sari* in a shop catches her eye, she will have a gloomy face when she comes home. You may ask yourself why she looks so unhappy. If you ask her why she is gloomy, she will tell you that she is lost in her thoughts over the *sari*. The only way to break the frown on her face is to buy her the *sari*. Until then all kinds of subtle discord will continue in the home. This is not how married life should be.

The wife may say to you, "I don't like the design of our sofas. The sofa your friend has is much nicer!" You ask, "You don't like our sofa anymore?" She will reply "No. Since I saw the other ones, I like them better." So now you buy her the sofa just like your friend's. But say that your child accidentally makes a cut into the sofa and when she sees the cut, she acts as if her soul has been cut. Children will cause damage, will they not? They even jump on the sofa, don't they? When they jump on the sofa she may cry out like they are jumping on her chest!

This is all *moha* (attachment). This *moha* will eat you alive and cause you to suffer.

This whole life of yours will be wasted away on such trivial things. Now I am telling all the ladies not to go shopping. They need to put a stop to all their shopping sprees. Just because you have the money, why do you buy things if you do not need to? It is all useless. Should you not be spending the money on something worthwhile? If someone has a hardship in his family and they do not have any money, wouldn't it be nice to give them fifty or hundred dollars? Why throw money away unnecessarily over things that create problems at home?

Questioner : Then the women throw terrible tantrums. They get crabby.

Dadashri : Men too throw terrible tantrums. Even I threw a terrible tantrum once, don't you know?

There are not a lot of tantrums nowadays. What is the purpose of throwing a tantrum? People throw tantrums because they want to have things their own way. By throwing a tantrum they intimidate and coerce the other person to give in or to make them act according to what they want.

Questioner : Why is it that in every situation, the women are blamed and not the men?

Dadashri : For women it is like this: The men used to control the laws so the women have been victimized.

Men have written most of the books and so the importance has been given to the husband. Women have not been given any recognition. These people have done away with any importance of women. Now, the men have also suffered in the process. These very men will be the ones who will go to hell. From here they go directly to hell. This is not so for women. They are spontaneous and natural by nature. They are not as awakened in spiritual matters as men are. The consequences they suffer are not as severe because of their nature.

Questioner : How long should one go on tolerating things?

Dadashri : Tolerance makes one stronger.

Questioner : So does that mean one just has to go on tolerating?

Dadashri : Instead of tolerating, it is better to think about things. Bring about a solution by thinking things through. It is wrong to tolerate. When there is too much tolerance, one bounces back like a loaded spring and when that happens, it creates chaos in the household. Tolerance is like a spring. One should not exert pressure on a spring, at any time. When you are dealing with other people, it is okay to an extent to use the spring, but as far as people in your own home are concerned, you should not exert any pressure on the spring. What will happen if you tolerate the people within your house? The spring will bounce back.

Questioner : What should be the limit for tolerance?

Dadashri : You should only be tolerant to a certain extent. You must then contemplate the facts involved. If you think profoundly, you will then come to realize the causes behind all the problems. If you just tolerate without thinking, the spring will bounce back. Therefore it is necessary to think. It is when one does not think, that he has to tolerate. If you think, then you will understand where the mistakes lie. That will bring about a solution. There is tremendous power within. Tremendous power! Whatever strength you ask for, will be granted. Unfortunately, people do not look for that strength within.

Instead they look for it on the outside. What strength is there on the outside?

It is because of tolerance that every household has disputes. People go around believing, "Look how much I have to tolerate." A solution has to be brought about by thinking things through. All events that come your way are nature's creations, so how will you escape them? If you want to settle your vengeances from your past lives and avoid creating new ones in your lives to come, you need to find a way out. The purpose of this current life is to unravel all revengeful ties from your previous life. You do this by settling all matters with equanimity, with everyone. Then your children will have such good upbringing.

Questioner : My friend has asked this question. Her husband is always getting angry with her, what is the reason behind this?

Dadashri : That is good, it is better that her husband, as opposed to others, gets angry. After all, he is one of your own. What do these blacksmiths do when they have a piece of steel they want to bend? They heat it and when it becomes bright red with heat, they hammer it so that it will bend. It can then molded into any shape desired. This example is applicable to human beings as well. If one gets hot, he becomes weak. The angrier he is, the weaker he becomes, making him more vulnerable to change. When he is weak, it takes little effort for the wife to form him in a way that is to *her* liking.

Questioner : Reform him into what, Dada? What does she do with him once he is under her control?

Dadashri : She can reform him how ever she pleases. She can turn her husband into a parrot. He will repeat whatever she says. He can become just like a parrot, but people do not know how to utilize their abilities. All these are weaknesses in people. To get angry is a weakness.

If while you were walking, a stone fell from the top of a building and hit you on the head, would you get angry?

Questioner : No, that just happens.

Dadashri : No, but why is it that you do not get angry in this situation? Because you do not see anyone involved here.

Questioner : No one has thrown the stone on purpose.

Dadashri : Therefore, we *do* have control over our anger. Once we know that no one has thrown the stone on purpose, we are able to control our anger. The control is definitely there. However, people say, "Anger overcomes me." That is wrong! Say that was true, why then do you remain calm in certain situations and get mad in other situations? If a policeman gets angry with you, why do you not get angry at him in return? You get angry with your wife, with your children, with the neighbours, and with those who work under you, but why don't you get angry with your boss? Anger does not overcome a man. It all occurs because he wants to do everything according to his own wishes.

Questioner : Whether it is at home or amongst friends, when things do not go according to our plan, due to differences of opinions, why do we get angry? What should we do about that?

Dadashri : What would happen if everyone tried to do things according to their expectations? How can one even afford to think like this? You should immediately realize that if everyone tried to do things their way, there would be nothing but chaos and conflict. At no point in time should you try to do things according to your expectations. If you do not have any expectations, you will never be disappointed. Having no expectations means that there isn't any need to fulfil anything. He who has needs, has expectations.

Questioner : What are we to do if, no matter how silent we remain, the men continue to get angry?

Dadashri : When he gets angry and you want to start a quarrel, then you too, should get angry, otherwise, you should put an end to it. If you want to stop the 'film,' then remain calm. If you don't want to stop the 'film,' then carry on fighting all night long. Who is preventing you? Do you like such 'films'?

Questioner : No I don't like such 'films'.

Dadashri : What is the use of getting angry? It is not the person who is getting angry, it is the alteration of the "mechanical adjustment" (the physical complex of thoughts, speech and actions that was charged in the past life) that initiates anger. He himself is not getting angry. Later on he regrets his anger.

Questioner : What is the solution to calm him down?

Dadashri : When a machine gets hot, you have to let it cool down. If you leave it alone for a little while it will eventually cool down. But if you disturb it or prod it, you will get burnt.

Questioner : My husband and I get into quarrels and verbal tiffs, what should we do?

Dadashri : Who gets angry first, you or him?

Questioner : He does, but then later on, I do too.

Dadashri : You have to scold yourself from within. Ask yourself why you are behaving in such a manner, and then remind yourself that in the end, you will have to suffer the consequences of your actions. With *pratikraman* all the transgression, will be erased. Otherwise, all the pushing and shoving you do will come back to bother you. Things will lose their intensity with *pratikraman*.

Questioner : But should there not be an occasional angry exchange between a husband and a wife?

Dadashri : No. There is no such law. There should be a lot of peace between a husband and a wife. If there is any hurt in the relationship, it cannot be considered a 'husband and wife relationship'. When even friends do not hurt eachother, how can a husband and wife do so? The friendship between a husband and wife is the highest friendship of all. Such a statement/belief (referring to the Questioner's question) is a way of justifying such behaviours. People who have altercations in their marriage use such a statement in order to justify their anger. Anger has no place at all between husband and wife.

Questioner : In our scriptures, it is written that a woman should treat her husband like the Lord. She is to obey and follow his commands. How can a woman apply this in this day and age?

Dadashri : Only if the husband is like Lord Rama, should she become like Sita. Now if he is belligerent and disgusting and behaves awkwardly, how is it going to work if you do not behave in the same manner? It would be superlative if you could live in harmony, but that is not feasible. How can the wife remain calm when he keeps pushing and prodding? What else is the poor wife to do? The husband should adopt a conduct that is becoming of an ideal husband and he should adopt conduct that is becoming of an ideal wife. If the husband makes a little mistake, she should endure it, but if he starts to abuse her, what is the poor woman to do?

Questioner : "The husband himself is The Eternal

Supreme Lord." What is wrong with this statement?

Dadashri : The husbands of today are such, that if they were considered as The Lord, they would go around like madmen.

Questioner : Can the husbands be called 'The Eternal Supreme Lords'? Should we do their *darshan* (look upon with devotion) everyday? Should we drink the water in which we bathe their feet?

Dadashri : You may address them as, 'The Eternal Supreme Lord', if they are immortal. How can you call them 'Eternal Supreme Lord' when they are going to die? How in heavens can the men of today be Lords?

Questioner : I bow down to my husband everyday.

Dadashri : You must be deceiving him by doing so. Women deceive men by prostrating in front of them. A husband is a husband and The Lord is The Lord. Where does the husband say "I am The Lord"? All he says is, "I am your boss." He says only this, does he not?

Questioner : Yes, he says only that.

Dadashri : Yes, even the cows have a boss; there is a boss for everyone and everything. The Soul is the only Lord, the Pure Soul.

Questioner : Should a woman drink the water (*charanamrut*), which is used to bathe her husband's feet?

Dadashri : How can you drink that water used on the men of today? They smell. Even when he sits there, he emits an odor. It was a different matter in the past, because people had a fragrance to them, but husbands today smell enough to give you a headache. Today you just have to play the role of a husband and wife whichever way you can.

Questioner : Dada, nowadays no one does this. Especially now that women are educated, they have discarded such practices.

Dadashri : The husbands are declared the Lord. Just look at them, they are the ones who wrote the books, so who is going to question them? They have turned everything on their side. It should not be this way.

Questioner : The women of today do not respect their husbands, as did the women of the past.

Dadashri : Yes, the husbands of the past were like Lord Rama and now they have become Mara! (Ma-ra opposite of Ra-ma) They have no qualities of Lord Rama.

Questioner : What is the wife's obligation towards her husband? Please explain this.

Dadashri : She should be sincere to her husband. The husband should tell his wife, "If you were to be insincere with me, then I would lose my head." You have to caution her. You have to tell her to beware, but do not pressure her into being sincere. You should remain sincere to each other all your life. Day and night, you should be thinking about him only. You should be concerned about him all the time. Only then will your life together run well.

Questioner : If the husband is not sincere and the wife loses her mind, will she bind karma?

Dadashri : If she loses her mind, they will both suffer. As much as possible, you should not lose your mind. If it was not the husband's intent to be insincere and he makes a mistake, then he should ask for forgiveness and reassure her that he will not make the same mistake again. A man has to be sincere does he not? How can things work when there is no sincerity?

Questioner : The husband repeatedly asks for forgiveness, but he also carries on the affair with his mistress. What then?

Dadashri : When the husband asks for forgiveness, can you not understand that he is suffering, with helplessness beyond his control? So you have to let go. It is not that he has acquired a habit of doing this. He has not become habituated. He too does not like it, but what can he do? These things happen against his will. Errors are made in this way, are they not?

Questioner : What should one do if the husband has become habituated to such marital infidelity?

Dadashri : What can you do? Can you throw him out? If you throw him out, there will be uproar in the community. On the contrary you have to keep it a secret. What else can you do? Do we keep our gutters covered or do we keep them open? Are these gutters to be kept covered or kept open?

Questioner : They have to be kept covered.

Dadashri : Otherwise if we keep them open, the foul stench will give you a headache.

Questioner : Why do the women wear *chandlo* (red dot in the center of the forehead)? Many American women ask me why Indian women wear *chandlos*.

Dadashri : This red dot in the middle of the forehead is very close to the inner mind and by wearing it, our women have the noble aim of keeping their mind only on their husband. These women will not leave or be insincere to their husband even if they have major clashes. The ones who traditionally do not have this *chandlo* may not remain sincere.

Questioner : Dada you have talked about how men should behave, but what should women do? What should women have in their two eyes?

Dadashri : A woman should accept her husband, no matter what he is like. The man she took as her husband is due to her own karmic account. It is by no coincidence that she married the man she did, so regardless of what her husband is like, she should make the effort to remain faithful to him. If she is not able to do so, then she should ask for his forgiveness. This however, should be her vision and she should think about how they both can progress spiritually. How they can both go into a higher life form in their next lives. How they can both attain liberation. This is what she should think about and focus on.

[20] RESULTS OF DIVORCE

Do you like differences of opinions? When there are differences in opinions, it will create discord. Excess discord results in a divorce.

Questioner : From the perspective of daily living, are our conflicts due to differences of opinions or differences in our thinking?

Dadashri : For all those who have not received the *Gnan* of Self realization, all differences are differences of opinions. For those who have self-realization, theirs is a difference in thinking. Differences in thinking do not cause hurt. A difference in opinion causes major conflicts and discord.

Questioner : Is it better to have a lesser difference of opinion?

Dadashri : People who aim to get along with each other

should not have any differences of opinion whatsoever. With such differences of opinions, discord and clashes will result, leading to loss of humility. Differences of opinions results in clashes and separation of inner oneness of minds, which in turn, leads to a miserable relationship and eventually a divorce.

Questioner : Our marriage is in trouble. We clash with eachother a lot. We are concerned. Please help us.

Dadashri : That is exactly what I am saying. It is not good. It does not look good to the world. There is no meaning in all this. There is still a chance for improvement. As long as you are in the human body, you have a chance to improve the situation. Why should it be like this anyway? Why create negative public scenes? You will have to understand a little bit at least, will you not? Do you understand? You have to be superficial in these matters. So many of you men have taken the role of a *dhani* (dominating husbands). You fools! Why are you behaving as if you own your wives? You are a husband only as long as you are living, or as long as you are not divorced. You could be divorced tomorrow. Then whom will you dominate?

Questioner : Nowadays, many people get divorced. They have small children, and the parents leave them. Are they not liable for the children's *nisaso* (the negative effects of children's grief on parents resulting in negative karmic bondage)?

Dadashri : Yes, they will be liable, but what can they do? Truly speaking they should not get divorced. Really they should tolerate each other for the sake of the children. It would not have mattered if they divorced before having children, but if they divorce after having children, they will have to suffer from their children's *nisaso*.

Questioner : If the husband has a mind that does not work and he does not do any work, he does not know how to run the motel; he just stays cooped up within the four walls of the house, so what then should be done?

Dadashri : What else can you do about it? There is no guarantee that you will find another one who is better than him.

Questioner : Yes that is for sure.

Dadashri : If the second husband is worse and if he abuses you, then what will you do? It happens to many women. Their first husbands were better by far and they were better off. Is it not necessary for people to understand this?

Questioner : If we leave it up to Dada, then will we get a better husband the second time?

Dadashri : He may turn out to be nice, but after three years he may have a heart attack, so what will you do then? This world is full of danger. It is better if you just tell yourself that things are meant to be the way they are and that you should accept whatever occurs. Accept it as correct. Accept it. That is better for you.

The first husband is generally good. The second is generally unfaithful. He is looking for something like this. He is wandering around looking for someone and she too is a wanderer, which is why they meet each other. It's like two wandering cattle coming together. Instead the first one is preferable. He may be useless, but at least you know what he was like. At least he will not strangle you in the night and you can be sure of that, whereas the second one may strangle you.

You should compromise just for the sake of the children. Even when there is only one child, he will become forlorn and unsupported if you divorce.

Questioner : Yes the children become without support.

Dadashri : Where is the mother? Where is the father? If a person loses his leg in an accident, will he not live without it for the remainder of his life, or will he commit suicide over it? In the same token put up with a crippled marriage.

You do not find your husband undesirable now, but when you do, what will you do? Even if he is not of a sound mind, you married him, and that makes him your husband. You should say, "Mine is the best of all." There is no such thing as a bad husband in this world.

Questioner : If we say he is the best, it would go to his head.

Dadashri : No it will not. The poor man works outside all day long, when does he have time to misbehave? Regardless of what your husband is like, you must accept him. Is it right for you to go out and get another one? Can you buy one? When you try to correct your situation by getting a divorce, it is not acceptable to the world. Other men will also ask whether she is a divorcee. So where else can you go? Instead just stick to one and settle your accounts. How many husbands do we change as Indians? This one that you have, whatever he is like, he is the real one, so deal with it and settle your account. As for men, whatever your wife is like, even if she fights and acts up, it is better to accept her. It is not as if she is eating you alive, she just keeps yelling and shouting at you. At least she is not physically abusing you. Really she is just a 'radio', but you are not able to truly understand all this. You may feel she is the one perpetuating the conflict, but later on even *she* regrets saying the things she did. Therefore, is she the one doing the talking or is it the radio?

In Bombay there was a lady whose marriage was falling apart. Her husband was secretly having an affair. When she found out, there were terrible rows at home. She came to me and told me what he was doing and asked me what she was to do. She wanted to break away. I told her that if she can find a husband who will be faithful to her completely then she might leave her current husband. Otherwise where was she going to find a better one? As such, her husband had only one mistress. I told her that was good under the circumstances. She should let go of the matter and she should keep an open mind because she would not find a better husband.

In this era, you cannot find a good husband or even a good wife. All these are trash and garbage goods. There are no good men or women to choose from. This current time is not meant for choosing, it is meant for settling past accounts. As far as you are concerned, you have to settle past accounts. But instead men and women are preoccupied in trying to behave as husband and wife. Instead people are complicating their accounts further by taking too much interest in their marriage. You pitiful people! You just have to settle everything here. Take the approach, which has the least amount of conflicts, and settle your accounts. There is not much time left.

Questioner : Dada, whatever events unfold, are they because of our past accounts?

Dadashri : Without account they would never meet.

As long as the world exists, there will be wounds. The wife will say that her wounds will never heal and yet she plunges back into the worldly life and the wounds do heal. This is what I call 'a stupor of fascination'. This fascination exists because of her *moha* (attachment to worldly life). Because of her *moha,* she forgets. It is because if this *moha* that her wounds heal. If these wounds did not heal, then one would get *vairaagya* (non-attachment to worldly things). What is the definition of *'moha'*? It is when many things have been experienced, but that experience is forgotten. While getting a divorce, a man decides that he will never marry again and yet he takes another desperate risk.

Questioner : I was telling her that ninety-nine percent of married couples are incompatible with each other.

Dadashri : Incompatibility amongst a couple in this era can work in two ways. It either elevates them spiritually or it will take them all the way down to lower life forms. Compatibility between couples can stagnate them both spiritually. It may even hurt them spiritually. An incompatible couple can make spiritual progress if they both use *Gnan* to prevent clashes.

Questioner : Under what circumstances is divorce justified?

Dadashri : These darn divorces are things that have just come about. Previously there was no such thing as a divorce.

Questioner : But nowadays they take place, so under which circumstances should one get a divorce?

Dadashri : If there is no possibility of harmony, then it is better to separate. If it is impossible to adjust, then it is better to separate. Otherwise, I say one thing only, "Adjust everywhere." Don't try to multiply things between the two of you by saying, "He's like this," and "She's like that."

Questioner : Are the divorces that take place in the west, when couples do not get along, considered bad?

Dadashri : What is the meaning of a divorce anyway? Are these people cups and saucers? When you cannot separate even a cup and saucer, how can you separate a man and a woman? It may be acceptable for the Americans, but you are an Indian. Once there used to be a vow of one wife, one husband. The kind of thinking, which prevailed, was that other than his own wife, a man would not even look at another woman. Where then do thoughts of divorce have any dignity in such a place? Do you like divorces?

In the animal kingdom, amongst the dogs, there are divorces and now amongst the humans as well. So how are humans and animals different? Man lives like a beast. In our Hindustan, there would not be another marriage after the first one. If the wife dies, the husband never remarries. What spiritual purity was possessed by the men born back then!

If a couple is on the verge of getting divorced, I will reunite them in one hour if you bring them to me. I will mend them in one hour, so they remain together again. All these problems are merely fears due to a lack of understanding. Many couples that were separated have now been happily reunited.

These are our moral values. Couples go on quarrelling and yet they stay together for eighty years. Even during the funeral rites on the thirteenth day, the widow would prepare everything that her late husband liked. She would even order food all the way from Bombay for the ceremony. A young boy would say to the old widow, "Maji, (title used to address elderly ladies), six months ago he pushed you and at that time you were calling him all kinds of names!" She would reply, "Even then, I would not find another husband like him." That is what the old widow would say. From the experiences of her entire life, she will discover that at heart, he was a nice man. His traits were awkward, but at heart he was good.

Our lives should be lived in such a way that people would take note of us. We are Indians, not Americans. We are such that, we abide by and endure the woman in our life, and the women are such, that women do the same. In this manner, eighty years together will pass. Foreigners do not tolerate even for an hour, neither he nor she would endure even for an hour.

The fireworks of everyone's *prakruti* are exploding. Where did these fireworks come from?

Questioner : They are an inherent trait in everyone.

Dadashri : You might be convinced that today there is going to be a big row, but instead it fizzles away. If your mind keeps tormenting you by saying over and over again, "He said so many things to me. So many horrible things happened today," then you should pat yourself on the back and tell yourself to go to sleep and that everything will be all right.

Did your wounds not heal? Is everything not fine now?

Questioner : When the quarrelling takes place, is it not the karmic baggage brought forward from the previous life that is coming out?

Dadashri : When fighting takes place, new karmic baggage is simultaneously being added for the next life. After receiving this *Gnan* however, only the old karmic baggage of the past life comes out. New baggage is not being filled.

Questioner : When my husband is quarrelling with me and I am doing *pratikraman*, is that a problem?

Dadashri : There is no problem.

Questioner : Does the karmic baggage come out during quarrelling?

Dadashri : Yes, all of it will come out. Wherever *pratikraman* is done, the baggage is coming out. *Pratikraman* is the only solution in this world.

What will you do from now on if your husband gets angry?

Questioner : Settle disputes with equanimity.

Dadashri : Is that so? Now will you leave him?

Questioner : No.

Dadashri : If he goes away, what will you do? What if he says he cannot stay with you?

Questioner : I would call him back. I would fall to his feet and ask for his forgiveness.

Dadashri : Yes, call him back. Appease him, stroke his hair, do whatever you have to. After that, things will settle down again. If a job can be done with just common sense, then use common sense. The next day, if he says "You were at my feet, begging me, were you not?" then that is a different matter. Then you can tell him, "Because you were leaving, you were acting like a mad person." He is under the impression that she will always plead and beg even though she only did it spontaneously to solve the problem at hand.

[21] THE ESSENCE OF THE SEVEN STEPS TAKEN IN THE MARRIAGE CEREMONY

There is no key for this day and age that shows you how to live your life. Forget about *moksh*, even then you need to know how to live your life, don't you? You just need to distinguish where each path leads, then decide which one you want to take. If you cannot decide, you must ask Dada, he will tell you which paths have perils along the way. Married people feel trapped in their marriage. Unmarried people feel that married people are blessed. Between the two, who will find the solution? It is hard to stay single in this world. One has no choice but to get married, so why be miserable in a marriage if you have no choice? Some question why they should get married and become miserable. This life is not meant for becoming miserable, but rather to acquire the experiences of this world; is this worldly life real or not? Is there happiness in it or not? This life is specifically meant for obtaining the basic meaning. Have you arrived at its meaning?

The relationship between a man and a woman is like that of a mill owner and the ox that turns the grinder. In India, there are small oil mills in the villages, where the ox is made to go round and round turning a mill, crushing and extracting oil from the seeds of a castor plant and other oil producing seeds. Parts of the ox's eyes are covered to restrict his vision in order to facilitate the process of repetitive walking in circles around the mill. The husband represents the bullock and the wife represents the bullock-master that runs the oil mill. They go around and around. The half-blinded ox thinks he must have covered a very long distance after a day of walking, but when his blinders are removed, he realizes that he is right where he started. Then what does the ox-master do? He feeds him a piece of oil cake and pleasing the bullock so that it starts working again. Similarly, the wife feeds her man a piece of *handavo* (savoury bread made from rice and lentils) and the husband eats peacefully and the whole labour of life resumes early the next morning.

It has become difficult now to pass days. When the husband comes home, he will complain about a pain in his chest and the children will come and announce they have failed their exams. When the husband has a pain in his chest, the wife will have anxieties about what is to become of her family if the husband has a heart attack. She will consume her mind with all kinds of negative thoughts, which will prevent her from living peacefully.

When can you say it is worth getting married? Only when just one person out of a hundred thousand gets married. What is the big deal when everyone marries? There is a big college (Dadashri's Science of worldly interaction) for women and men where they can learn how to conduct their life's interactions after marriage, but these people get married without educating themselves.

If someone insults you there is no problem in accepting the insult, but you have to keep that insult in your awareness and remind yourself, "Is this life meant for such insults?" There is no problem with insults, there is no need for anything that elevates the ego, nor is there a need for anything that defeats the ego, but is our life meant for insults? Should we not have this awareness?

As long as the wife is sulking, he would say, "Oh God, please help me!" When she comes back to talk to him, he forgets everything, and God and everything else is set aside. How intense is this puzzle? Is your suffering going to heal this way?

What is the meaning of this world? Troubles. Even this body is trouble. Should there be a desire for troubles? It is a wonder indeed that there is any desire for this. A fishing net is different from the worldly life net. With a fishnet, you can at least cut your way through and escape, but you cannot escape from the net of this worldly life. Even when you die, you do not escape.

A *Gnani Purush* shows you a way to escape the net of the world. He shows you the path to *moksh* (liberation) and puts you on that track so that you feel that you have been liberated from the problems of external forces forever.

How can you call this a life? How lovely life should be! Each and every person should emit a fragrance. There would be praises sung all around, about how wonderful a person is, how nicely he talks, and how wonderful his conduct is. Do you see anyone around you with this kind of a reputation? Do you see people with such fragrance around you?

Questioner : Rarely do some people emit such a fragrance.

Dadashri : Perhaps some people may, but by how much? If you ask the people in his home, they will say he stinks. He may have a fragrance outside but at home they will say, "Don't even talk about him." That is not called fragrance.

Life should be spent helping others. Does the incense stick enjoy its own fragrance when it is burning?

This world is a museum, what are the requirements of this museum? When you enter the museum, you are free to enjoy and do as you please within the rules while inside, but once you leave you are to leave all of its belongings behind. Such is the case with this world. You are not to take anything away. Do not fight. Do not create attachment or abhorrence with anyone. People, however, enter and get married. You fool! Why did you get married? You got married because you developed an attachment. On your way out, this will become a problem. Then he will complain, "I am bound." It is still not a problem if you go inside and follow the rules. You can eat, drink and enjoy. If you happen to get married tell your wife that it is a museum; you should not get attached or develop any ill feelings towards each other. As long as it is convenient, have fun but in the end you should leave without any attachments, positive or negative. You should not have any negative feelings or abhorrence toward her even if she goes out with another man. This is what this museum of life is like. Do whatever you want to, but now it is too late to get rid of this museum. Whatever has happened so far, so be it. We are born in a country of high morals. Therefore, marriage and everything else must be as it was meant to be, orderly and just.

[22] DIFFERENCES IN THE INTRINSIC QUALITIES OF MEN AND WOMEN

Questioner : Can women attain knowledge of the Self? Can they achieve a state of Self-realization and an enlightened worldview?

Dadashri : Really it is not possible, but my science makes it so that they too, become Self-realized. This is because their *prakruti* (complex of thoughts, speech and acts) itself, is such that it is not conducive for knowledge of the Self. Women have much higher amount of deceit and *moha* (fascination which makes one forget their real nature; the force that makes one forget after suffering) in their *prakruti*, which prevents them from attaining knowledge of the Self as easily as men.

Questioner : Then isn't that injustice by *vyavasthit* (natural law, scientific circumstantial evidence)?

Dadashri : No, she will become a man in her next life and then she will attain *moksh*. This common knowledge that women cannot attain liberation is not entirely untrue. It is true when you take into account the nature of women. The elements of deceit and *moha* simply impede Self-realization. It is untrue when one says that a woman is simply never going to be liberated. She becomes a man and then attains *moksh*. There is no law that women will remain as women in their next life. When will she become like a man? It is when she remains in competition with a man in this life and her ego and anger continue to increase, and the atoms of deceit and *moha* in her, decrease. Men's *prakruti* is predominantly that of *ahankar* (ego) and *krodh* (anger), while women's *prakruti* is of *maya* (attachment) and *lobh* (greed). This is how it has been carrying on naturally, but our *Akram Vignan* says that women too, can achieve *moksh* because this science awakens the Soul and many women are such, that they constantly remember Dada twenty-four hours a day.

Many women in India and America have Dada on their mind, twenty-four hours a day.

Questioner : The Soul does not have any gender right?

Dadashri : The Soul does not have a gender. The *prakruti* has a gender. If you have a stock of 'shining goods', then 'shining goods' will come out, and if you have a stock of 'dark and dingy goods', then that is what will come out. *Prakruti* too, is a stock that is stored within. It is called *'pudgal'* (body). So whatever was taken in (*puran*), continues to dissipate (*galan*). Eating food is *puran*, going to the bathroom is *galan*. Eating, going to the bathroom, and breathing are all acts of *pudgal parmanu* (the atoms of the physical body. *Pudgal* = body. *Parmanu* = subatomic particle that cannot be further divided).

If one wants to be a *purush* (man), it will happen when the stocks of *moha* (attachment) and *kapat* (deceit) go away. When these two *parmanus* (atom complexes) of *moha* and *kapat* unite, a woman is formed, and when *krodh* (anger) and *maan* (pride) unite, a man is formed. Everything (the formation of human bodies) takes place according to the science of atoms (*parmanus*).

Once, a few ladies admitted to me that they have certain major faults and wanted to know which of all their faults, was the most detrimental to them? I told them the most detrimental fault women have is to make others behave according to their expectations. Every woman has a desire to make others do what she wants. She even manages to change her husband by means of deceit, and then makes him do what she wants. This is wrong. It is a wrong approach. I have asked the women to write me a promise that they will not do this. What is the reason for making someone comply with your own expectations? It is very harmful.

Questioner : If it benefits the family, then what is wrong with it?

Dadashri : No. One is never able to do any good with this approach. Those women, who do things only according to their expectations, never do any good for their family. The family only benefits if things happen according to everyone's expectations. It only happens if no one is hurt in the process. Those who go around making everyone do things according to their own expectations, are doing great damage to their family. This is the primary cause of conflicts and quarrels. If things do not go according to her expectations, then she sits around sulking and she will not eat. Who can she beat up? So she sits there shouting. Then the next day she will employ deceit. What kind of a woman is that? What would happen if you did not get your way? You ladies should not insist on these things. You need to become broadminded and big-hearted.

Questioner : Women soften their husbands through their tears and even if they are wrong, they will insist they are right. What do you have to say regarding this matter?

Dadashri : That is very true. She will have to pay for her wrongdoing. Furthermore, she loses credibility by acting this way. She will lose the trust of her husband.

I asked a group of ladies, "Tell me whose husband is naïve? Raise your hand." All the ladies who raised their hands, told me in confidence, "My husband is naive, totally naive." This statement in itself shows that these women play with their husbands as if they were toys. It looks bad to expose this matter in public. Does it not look bad? One cannot say everything openly. If I ask the ladies confidentially, "Is your husband naive?" They will respond, "Very naive, very naive." Their deceit makes them see him as naive. This deceit is bad. Nevertheless, there are many other good qualities in women.

Questioner : On the one hand, a woman is called 'Laxmi' (Goddess of wealth and prosperity) and on the other hand, she is called deceitful and is said to be filled with *moha* (attachment to worldly things).

Dadashri : They can be called Laxmi. Women are no ordinary beings. If her husband is called Narayan (The Lord), then what does that make her? Therefore, the pair is called 'Laxminarayan'! Does that make her worthless? She is the mother of a *Tirthankar*. Who gave birth to those twenty-four *Tirthankars*?

Questioner : A woman.

Dadashri : So then, how can you call women worthless? *Moha* will always be there because she is a woman. However, who gave birth to all the great *Tirthankars*? It is women who give birth to all the elevated people, so how can we disgrace them? Yet, our people disgrace them.

Questioner : It is always the women who are told to remain within the boundaries, not the men.

Dadashri : That is a misuse as a human being. It is a misuse of the authority one has as a human being. Authority can be used in two ways; it can either be used appropriately or it can be abused. If used properly, people will be happy, but if one abuses it, he will have miseries. When you misuse authority, you will lose that authority. If you want to maintain the authority forever, if you want to remain a man forever, then do not abuse your authority. Otherwise, you will become a woman in your next life. All you people of authority beware because abuse of authority, will result in loss of that authority.

The epitome of a woman is a woman who, regardless of what may happen to her, if her husband is by her side or not, if her husband has run away, she would not run off with another man. Regardless of what the other man may be like, even if God comes to her as a man, she would refuse to go with him. She would say, "No, I have a husband, I am married!" That is called a *sati* (a woman who is unconditionally devoted to her husband, so much that she would voluntarily give up her life on her husband's funeral pyre). Are there any qualities of a *sati* left in these women nowadays? It is not as if there have never been such women. The times are different. There are certain periods like that of *Satyug* (the time cycle of golden ages), when *satis* were to be found. That is why people revere and worship *satis,* don't they?

Questioner : Yes.

Dadashri : It is because they have the desire to become a *sati*. If someone ever thinks or utters the name of a *sati*, one day they could become one and yet sex (*vishaya*) is sold at the price of bangles (cheap, i.e. it is 'dime a dozen'). Do you know that? Do you understand what I am saying?

Questioner : Yes, it is sold at the price of bangles.

Dadashri : In which market is sex for sale? In the colleges! At what price? Sex is sold at the price of gold. Some will be sold at the price of diamonds. It is not like this everywhere. Some women will not accept even gold, no matter what you give them, they will not concede. However, other women will allow themselves to be bought; these women of today, it may not be at the price of gold, but at some other price.

Therefore, it is because of sex that he has become a woman. Man has encouraged and corrupted women because of his lust for sex. Even if she has no meritorious qualities, she believes she is special because men will encourage her and compliment her for their own desires. Why does she believe this? She believes this because this is what men have persistently been telling her. It is not something that she will come to believe on her own, but because the men are telling her over and over again, she thinks it must be true. If you were to tell a woman she is very nice and that no other woman is comparable to her, she will believe you, even if she is ugly. If you tell her she is very beautiful, then she will believe herself to be beautiful. Men have kept women as women. All along in this game, the women in their mind believe they are making fools of men. In this way, men get their lust satisfied after which, they leave them.

Questioner : It is not written that a woman will remain a woman for many lives to come. Women do not know this fact and that is why they do not look for a solution.

Dadashri : If the problem is solved, then a woman is actually a man. Unfortunately, these women do not know the root cause. Furthermore, they enjoy their role as women. They take pleasure in being women and that is why they remain as one and nobody knows the way out, so no one can show them the way out. Only the women, who were *satis*, knew the way out. A *sati* would never even think about another man except her husband, even if her husband were to die immediately after their marriage or if he were to run away. She would believe her husband to be the only man for her. Deceit in such women would melt away.

If a woman becomes like a *sati,* her deceitful tendencies will begin to disappear. Those prominent *satis* (of the past) were born as *satis* because they were not tainted from their past lives. Whereas for you, there are stains from the past life and so the next time you will be born a man. However, having been born a man, realize that not all men are equal. Many men are like women. They have a few characteristics of a woman (e.g. deceit). If this deceit disappears either by becoming a *sati* or by acquiring Self-realization through meeting a *Gnani Purush*, then a woman will attain liberation. In becoming a *Sati*, everything will be clear and then he or she will attain *moksh*. Do you understand a little of what I am saying? On the way to liberation, every woman has to become either a *Sati*, or a man. Men are very naive; they will do whatever is asked of them. Women have taken advantage of all men. Of all the women, only a *Sati* would not do so. A *sati* would regard her husband as her lord.

Questioner : You see a very few people with this kind of a life.

Dadashri : How can there be such lives in this *Kaliyug* (current time cycle of lack of unity in thoughts, speech and acts)? Even in *Satyug* (time cycle of truth and unity of thought, speech and acts) there were very few *Satis*. So how can there be any in *Kaliyug*?

So the women are not at fault; women are like goddesses. The soul is the soul, whether it be in form of a man or a woman, the only difference is of the packing, the physical body. Being a woman is an effect of a kind and this effect works on the Soul because of the presence of ignorance. With the knowledge of the Self, this effect of a woman does not work on the Soul. This is liberation. Woman is a *shakti* (power, energy). In this country many women have been great in government and politics. Imagine her potential in the field of religion. They have the power to liberate the world. Women are a store of energy for the salvation of the world. She has enough energy to achieve her own liberation and help others achieve the same.

[23] WHEN SEX STOPS, LOVE STARTS

When does a married life become radiant? It is only when both the husband and the wife have a fever (Dada is referring to sexual relationship) that they take medicine (have sex). Would anyone take medicine without having a fever? If sexual activity takes place when one of the partners does not have a desire for it, then that married life does not shine. You should take the medicine only if you both have the fever. This is the only medicine. Just because the medicine is sweet, it does not mean you have to take it every day. For a marriage to be harmonious the man needs to control his passion for sex. All these animals have no control over passion. All great men and women of the past, like Rama, Sita, and others, had control over their passions. Lack of control is a bestial quality. This world is not aware of the dangers of sex. In just a single sexual act, five hundred thousand lives are destroyed at a time. Because people do not understand this, they continue to enjoy sex. They do not realize this. Only under extreme situations, which become beyond your control, should sex occur.

Every religion has created the confusion that man has to leave the woman (for spiritual progress). Then where would I go if I did that? Who will cook for me? Should I be running my business or should I be cooking at home?

Scriptures and religions have praised the married life; they have not condemned it. They have condemned infidelity and immorality.

Questioner : Is sex only meant for procreation or can it be enjoyed through the use of birth control?

Dadashri : No, no. That was in the past, during the times of sages and ascetics. In those days the relationship between the husband and the wife was not like it is today. The sages used to marry, but generally they avoided marriage. The prospective wife would argue with him that he would not be able to live properly on his own and would ask him to have a partnership with her. By doing so, they would be able to maintain their religious practices and their devotional rituals while, at the same time maintain their daily life. Some sages and ascetics accepted such proposals, but they would tell their wives that they would not have a family with them. The wives would agree on the condition that they are given a gift of one son and one daughter from them, thereafter there would be no sexual relationship between them and they would live as friends. The ascetics would accept those terms and then they would live together as friends and not as husband and wife. She would take care of all the duties of the home and he would take care of things outside the home. Later, they would sit together to devote their time for spiritual practice. But nowadays, sex has become the main pastime; it has become a business and consequently everything has become ruined. The ascetics were very controlled and wise.

Even now if the union in the marriage is for a son and a daughter, there is nothing wrong with it. Then if husband and wife should live together as friends, they will not encounter any misery in their lives. But instead they look for happiness in sex and then they start to make demands on each other. The ascetics were a different kind of people.

Do you vow to remain absolutely sincere to your wife? If you say yes, then liberation is yours, but you lose that right to liberation the moment you start thinking about other women, because you are indulging in something that is not yours by right. If you take what is yours by right, then there is liberation for you, but if you take anything or enjoy anything that you have no right to, you will be doomed for the animal life.

There are limitations to sex between a man and a woman. What are these limitations? There should be no sexual contact or relationship with anyone other than your spouse. If you have sexual thoughts about other men or women, you should do *pratikraman* and wash them away. The most ominous danger that exists is that of taking pleasure with someone else's wife or husband. There is no danger with your own wife. Now am I doing anything wrong here? Am I scolding you in any way? Is there anything wrong here? This is my scientific discovery. As far as the ascetics are concerned, there is a special rule for them. They are told not to look at even a statue of a woman. They are not to sit in the same place a woman had been sitting. However, I have not placed such restrictions have I?

In the current time cycle, if you have a sexual relationship with only your spouse, then I consider that as an act of celibacy (*bramcharya*). If you remain sincere to your spouse, then the benefits you reap from doing so, will be equivalent to the benefits one received when practising the level of celibacy (no sex at all) required during the time of the *Tirthankars* (The Absolute and Fully Enlightened Lords).

Questioner : Does this sincerity apply to only physical acts or does it also include the subtle, internal thoughts also, as the mind is such that it cannot refrain from wandering?

Dadashri : Your sincerity is also required at the subtle level. It should also be at the thought level and if the mind wanders at times, remain detached from the mind, but for that you have to keep doing *pratikraman*. What is the condition for liberation? It is the vow of one wife and one husband. Vow of true monogamy for both a man and a woman will give them liberation.

If you are married then enjoy sex with your wife, which

is rightfully yours. If you indulge in carnal activities with anyone other than your spouse, the consequences will be very grave indeed.

If you leave your own wife and have an affair with some other woman, then in your next life you will have to roam wherever that woman roams. If she goes into lower life forms or a non-human form, then you will have to go there too. She will take you there with her. Nowadays, this is what happens everywhere. There is no telling where your next birth will be. Anyone, who indulges in forbidden sexual relationships, will have to endure tremendous physical and mental suffering. Even their daughter will have immoral characteristics in just one rebirth. The law of nature is such that, with whomever you had violated the rules of rightful sex, that very woman will become your mother or your daughter in your next life. The moment you violate the rules, you lose your right to be born as a human in the next life. It is a tremendous sin. When you enjoy someone else's wife, then others will enjoy your daughter. Who cares about this in these times?

There are always *kashayas* (anger, pride, attachment, greed) in forbidden sex, and wherever there is *kashaya*, one has to go to hell (life filled with severe incessant suffering). However, people are not aware of these consequences and that is why they do not have any fear. They are not afraid of anything. Your current human life is the reward of your good deeds from your past life.

Sex arises out of attraction, and ultimately leads to repulsion. When repulsion takes place, vengeance is created and vengeance is the foundation of this world.

Money is a cause of vengeance. Ego is a cause of vengeance. Sex is a cause of vengeance. Of these three causes, sex is the most poisonous.

It is sex and sexual desires that are the root cause. Out of your sexual desire arises delusion and this delusion destroys *Gnan*. Sex is the biggest obstacle; it is the root cause that deludes you. Delusion creates desire for wealth and excess wealth exacerbates the ego. If sexual desires dissipate, all else vanishes.

Questioner : So we should know how to destroy the seed, the root cause, but how can we do that?

Dadashri : It can be done through the process of *pratikraman*; through *alochana* (recalling mistake), *pratikramam* (repent for wrongdoing), and *pratyakhyan* (decision not to repeat it).

Questioner : That is all? Is there no other solution?

Dadashri : There is no other solution. If you do *tap* (penance) then you bind good karma. And by destroying the root cause, you get results; you become free form the entanglements of karma. What does the law of settling with equanimity state? It states that you must make sure that you do whatever you can to prevent binding vengeance with the other party. Become free from vengeance.

Questioner : How does the binding of vengeance take place? How are the seeds of vengeance from countless previous lives, planted?

Dadashri : You will not bind vengeance with a dead man or a dead woman. Vengeance is bound through interactions with the living beings.

Questioner : Why does that happen?

Dadashri : It is because of differences of opinions. You may want to go to a movie whereas she may want to go to a play. The "timing" does not match. So marry only if the "timings" match, (i.e. only get married if you are compatible).

All the happiness that you have derived from this dependency on sex as a means of pleasure is all borrowed happiness; it is on loan to you, and because it is a loan, you will have to pay it back.

You are not enjoying the happiness of the Soul, but instead you have asked for happiness from the body. There is no problem if you take happiness from the Soul, but you have borrowed it from the body and so you will have to pay it back. This is a loan. Whatever pleasure you derived from that loan, you will have to repay by an equivalent amount of suffering. Whatever has been borrowed from the body will have to be paid back to the body.

Some people tell me their wives make them beg for sex. I tell them, "You fool! What do you expect when you have no dignity left?" By doing this you have nothing left. Smarten up and become a *Yogi* (ascetic).

One woman would make her husband prostrate in front of her four times before she would let him touch her. You imbecile! Why not commit suicide instead? Why don't you take a terminal dip in the ocean? At least the ocean is straight forward, and there won't be any problems there. You prostrate four times for this?

Questioner : In the past life I probably had clashed with her. In this she has clashes with me. We will have to find a way out of this. What is the solution?

Dadashri : There is a solution for it, but people are mentally weak. The solution is to stop the inclination towards sex. Only then will everything else stop automatically. All the arguments continue because of your inclination for sexual pleasure.

Questioner : Now how can we do this? How can we stop it now?

Dadashri : Conquer sex.

Questioner : It is because we are not able to conquer sex that we are here at your feet.

Dadashri : Sex for so many years. Sex even in your old age? Wherever you see it is sex, sex and sex.

Questioner : We have stopped but our quarrelling has not ceased, that is why we are at your feet, Dada.

Dadashri : That can never be. I have seen that wherever sex has stopped, wherever men have become strong willed, wherever their minds have become strong, their wives absolutely abide by what they say.

There is no other solution other than stopping sex with your wife. The root cause of attachment and abhorrence is sex. The original, main cause is sex. This is the starting point of the world. Therefore, if a person wants to stop this cycle of recurrent worldly life, then he has to stop sex.

People who do not want any clash and who do not side with quarrelling, for them the quarrelling will continue to occur but it will gradually decrease. But as long as one believes that clashes are necessary, then clashes will continue to increase. We should not support any quarrelling or clashes. Those who have made a firm decision not to be involved in clashes, will encounter very few clashes. Wherever there is clash, God is not present.

You need to put a stop to this system of double beds and keep single beds and sleep separate from each other in your own single beds.

From the time my sexual interactions stopped with my

wife, I have been addressing her as 'Hiraba'. Since that time, we have not had any difficulties. The difficulties we had before were primarily in regards to sex, but we also used to have trivial minor arguments. These trivial arguments remained as long as the sting of sex was present. I am telling you from my personal experience. We have this *Gnan* of ours and because of it, we are saved, but otherwise if this *Gnan* were not there, this sting of sex would keep on biting you. At that time, I had ego.

Just look at this science. All conflicts with the whole world will stop. All clashes with the wife and children will also stop. This science is such that the conflicts stop and you become free.

[24] MYSTERY BEHIND MEETING EACH OTHER LIFE AFTER LIFE

Marriage is a major bondage. It is like being locked up as cattle in a carriage. It is best not to be trapped in that situation. But if you happen to get married, it is in your best interest to settle all your accounts of the relationship with equanimity. If not, then in the end, get out after having tasted its fruits. In reality the Soul is not anyone's husband or wife, man or son. It is only karma that are unfolding and accounts that are being settled. The Soul remains unchanged in all this. The Soul is the soul and the Absolute Self is Absolute. It is your belief that she is your wife.

Who teaches these birds how to weave such beautiful nests? You will not have to put too much effort in how to run your daily life. Yes there is some effort required in acquiring knowledge of the Self. However, there is no need to do anything to run this world. Of all the living things, only humans think that they are too smart. Do these animals not have spouses? Do they have to get their children married? It is only these humans who end up having wife and children; only the human beings are so caught up with marriages.

Even these cows and buffaloes have marriages; they too have children, but is there such thing as a husband (boss) there? They too become fathers-in-law and mothers-in-law, but do they organize things like these 'intelligent' people? Do they ever say, "I am her father-in-law?" Despite this their lives are just like ours. They too, breast feed their young, and lick their calves don't they?

You are a pure Soul and your interactions with the world should be superficial. You have to remain in the 'home department' (your real Self) and remain superficial in the 'foreign department' (your relative self). Superficial means not having tendencies to get involved or engrossed in thoughts, speech, and acts. Live your life as if you are in a drama, but this drama has to be acted out very precisely; at the time of profit you have to laugh in this drama and at the time of losses, you have to cry. You have to accurately portray the emotions in the drama. You have to act out the part, but do not become involved internally. We have to maintain casual acquaintances and connections only. Have you not heard people say, "My relationship with this gentleman is casual"? That is the kind of relationship you have to keep with the whole world. He, who knows how to maintain this kind of a relationship, becomes a *Gnani*. You have to keep a similar relationship even with your body. I have that kind of a relationship with everyone, but people still tell me, "You keep very good relationship with us." I go through the motion of all the worldly interactions while remaining as the Self.

Questioner : Is it possible that a husband's success is because of his wife's good karma? Don't people say that it is because of the wife's good karma that the family has wealth and prosperity? Is that true?

Dadashri : People say those things to keep an abusive husband in check. If a man abuses his wife, then people around will tell him, "Just look at the good fortune of your wife. Why are you abusing her? You are able to eat because of her good karma." That is how everything got started. Each living being eats due to its own karma. Do you understand? However, you have to say these things, because only then will things move along. Everyone enjoys the fruits of their own merit karma and the suffering they have to endure is also due to their own bad karma. In reality, no living being ever interferes with another living being. There is absolutely no interference of any kind whatsoever.

Questioner : If a man does some charitable work and his wife supports this, do both of them reap the benefits of the good deeds?

Dadashri : Of course! The person who carries out the task, the one who encourages him to do so, and the person who supports that task, are all collectively involved and therefore they will all reap the benefits of the good deed. If someone tells you, "Do this because it is a worthwhile task," and you follow his advise, you become the 'doer', he becomes the one to encourages the task, and if your wife does not object to it, she becomes the supporter. All three will bind karma. The doer will reap fifty percent of the benefits and the remaining fifty percent will be distributed between the one who encouraged the task and the one who supported it.

Questioner : What should one do to be free from the karmic relations created from past life?

Dadashri : You end up living with a person because of your past life account. If you simply do not like living with the person you are married to, you have no choice. This is your account and you cannot escape it. So then, what should you do? You should keep relations with that person on the outside, but from within you should do *pratikraman* for them, because your current predicament is a result of your *atikraman* (causes, transgression of attachment or abhorrence through the mind, speech or actions) from your past life. What were the causes? The causes were acts of transgression against that person in your previous life, the result of which you are now experiencing. Therefore if you do *pratikraman* for him, you will lighten the load. Keep doing *pratikraman* internally and keep asking for forgiveness from his Soul. Then you will be able to bring an end to your misery. Do your *pratikraman* through any God and keep that God as your witness, then everything will be cleared, otherwise what will happen? If you keep looking at him with scorn and you keep blaming him, contempt will set in and you will come to hate him. Feelings of hate and contempt will lead to feelings of aversion and fear. When you feel contempt for a person, you will also fear that person. The moment you see that person, you feel afraid. Recognize this as a consequence of inner contempt. In order to be free from contempt, repeatedly keep asking for forgiveness from the pure Soul of the person you have contempt for. This contempt will stop in two days. Acknowledge your faults and all wrongdoing against that person. Understand that your current predicament is the result of your own past errors. Ask the Lord within him, for forgiveness for all the hurt you have caused him. Then everything will be washed away.

Questioner : If we want to follow the path of religion, then we have to renounce our home and the world. This may be good for our religious progress, but it hurts the people at home. Is it not selfish to renounce the life at home for one's own religious benefit?

Dadashri : First you will have to fulfil your obligations and responsibilities towards your family. If you make them happy, then they will be happy to let you to go without any reservations. However, do not do anything that would hurt them because you cannot breach that agreement.

Questioner : I feel like leaving this material world, what should I do?

Dadashri : Do you admit that there was a day when you had a desire to be part of this material world?

Questioner : At that time I did not have this *Gnan*, now I do. It makes all the difference.

Dadashri : Yes, it does make a difference, but now that you have entered into it, you have to find a way out. However, you cannot just run away from it.

[25] YOU WILL NOT MEET THE SAME PARTNER LIFE AFTER LIFE

Questioner : When one partner's karmic account is paid off, they pass on to another life. When that occurs, are we likely to meet that individual again? If that individual has created an account with us, are we likely to meet them again in another life?

Dadashri : If an account is bound with them, you will meet them again. If you forget the world by just looking at the person, then the karmic bond has already been created. "My one and only son, I cannot live without him." So what will you do when you have to go to cemetery (die)? Never speak that way; do not say, "He is my one and only son." When the time comes to go, he will go. A crematorium and cemetery are the businesses of this world. People take birth, but death is inevitable.

Questioner : Precious time is passing away.

Dadashri : Death is inevitable. You are going to die even as you insist that she is yours. Really she is not yours, and if she goes early, then you have to sit alone. If she really was yours, you both would depart together, would you not? At times a rare woman becomes a *Sati* (one who voluntary dies on the husband's funeral pyre) with her husband, but even then what path will she take and what path will he take? Each individual's future life form is dependant upon his karmic account. Some will be born again as humans while some will go into the animal kingdom. Some will become celestials. A *Sati* will claim, "If I die with him, I will be born with him." However, that does not happen. That is all foolishness. Really there is no such thing as a husband and wife. All these unions are 'arrangements' made by society.

Questioner : If there are no quarrels in a marriage, then will a husband and wife be able to live together again in the next life?

Dadashri : In this very life, there is no harmony together. Couples divorce each other in this very life, so why are you even talking about the coming life? There is no such love at all. Those who are likely to be together in the next life are couples that have harmony in this current life. They have a lot of love in their life. They do not see any faults in each other at all. If either one of them makes a mistake, the other will not see it as such; this is the kind of love that exists between the two.

Questioner : If their present life is filled with such love, then will the same people come together in their next life?

Dadashri : Yes they can; certain lives are such that they will. If they have never quarrelled in their entire life, then they will come together again.

[26] IDEAL INTERACTIONS IN MARRIED LIFE

Dadashri : What is the method to improve life?

Questioner : To go on the right path.

Dadashri : For how long should you try to improve your life, how many years, how many days, how many hours? How will it improve?

Questioner : I don't know.

Dadashri : Aha! That is why it does not improve. Really you only need to work to improve two days. First improve your working day and second, improve your holiday. Only two days need to be improved from the morning to night. If you change these two around, all others will change. If you make changes and arrange them in a certain way, then the rest will follow. You don't have to make changes over a long period of time. Only these two days need to be organized. When these two days are organized, all the rest will automatically be included.

Questioner : How do you make these arrangements?

Dadashri : When you wake up in the morning, finish whatever prayers you want to do. You should make it a custom to wake up early in the morning. Aim to wake by five in the morning and then for half an hour, devote your time to meditate on higher things. If you have a religion that you follow, then perform your devotional duties for the next half hour. This should then carry on everyday. Then get up and brush your teeth, etc. Have a systematic approach even when you are brushing your teeth. Fetch your own toothbrush; do everything yourself. You should not ask anyone for anything. It is a different matter if you are sick. After tea and breakfast, you may suggest to your wife that, since there was not enough sugar in the tea, then perhaps tomorrow she can add a little more.

Just make her aware of it, but don't start quarrelling. After breakfast, go to work and fulfil your duties there.

Leave your home without any quarrels, and if you have a conflict at work with your boss then settle your mind on the way home. Leave your work problems, at work. Enter your home with a quiet mind. Do not have any disputes in the home. If you fight with your boss, what fault is it of your poor wife? Do you have disagreements with your boss or not?

Questioner : I do.

Dadashri : Then what fault is it of your wife? When you come home after fighting with your boss, then she'll know that you are not in a good mood. Does that happen?

Questioner : Yes.

Dadashri : So organize one working day in this manner and one holiday. There are only two different kinds of days. There is not a third kind of a day is there? So organize these two days, and then things will move along.

Questioner : Now what should we do for a holiday?

Dadashri : On your day off, you should take your family for an outing, since they do not go out much. Have a nice meal at home, make good food, and then take them out. Limit your expense when you go out. If sometimes you have to spend extra money, then you can budget it out, but limit your expenses. Decide all this with the approval of your wife. Let your wife make the decisions.

Questioner : She'll say eat *vedhami* (sweet bread) at home and do not go out and eat pizza.

Dadashri : Eat *vedhmi* joyfully. Eat everything. Eat *dhokra*, eat *jalebi*, eat whatever you like.

Questioner : But we should not eat pizza at a restaurant outside?

Dadashri : Eat pizza? How can we eat pizza? We uphold the practice of purity in food. Despite this, if you are really fond of it, eat several times, but gradually stop it. Do it very slowly and gradually. If you put a stop to it suddenly, that is wrong. You should eat along with everyone and then gradually stop it.

Questioner : What should I do if the wife does not enjoy cooking it?

Dadashri : Then change your preference to other dishes. There are many varieties of dishes. Change your preferences. If you don't like a certain flavour, then have her change the spices to your liking. What is there to eat in a pizza?

If you organize your life in this manner, it will run smoothly. In the morning, if you devote half an hour to your prayers and devotional singing, then things will fall into place. You have received *Gnan* already, so now you have become wise. However, those who do not have *Gnan*, will need to do some *bhakti*. But as for you, you are on the right path.

This *Akram Vignan* does not interfere with your daily life. All other forms of religious or spiritual knowledge have relative contempt for the worldly life. This Science does not offend the worldly life in the least bit. It remains within the confines of its 'reality' and does not offend anything at all.

The ultimate 'light' (knowledge) is where not even a single being is hurt in the slightest degree. Even the opponent will become pacified and they will say, "We have our differences but at the same time I have a lot of respect for you." They will say such good things. However the opposition will always be there. There is opposition against the *Gnani* as well as the fully enlightened *Tirthankar*. Therefore there will always be opposition. Not everyone has the same viewpoints. Not everyone can be on the same level of thinking.

At home, your interactions should be filled with harmony. Your wife should feel that she will never find a husband like you and you should feel like you will never find a wife like her. When this happens your life together is considered worthy.

Questioner : There is no parallel to your talks of spirituality, but your talks about the worldly life are also second to none; they are extraordinary Dada.

Dadashri : It is like this; no one has been able to attain liberation without understanding the worldly life as it is. No matter how priceless the knowledge of the Self is, without understanding the worldly life, no one has attained liberation. That is because the world has to let you go. If it does not, then what will you do? You are a pure Soul for sure, but the world has to let you go also. Instead, you go around complicating your worldly life even more. So now (after *Gnan*), bring about an end and solve your worldly problems as quickly as possible.

Jai Sat Chit Anand

PRAYER TO PURESELF

Oh Pure Soul within me! You reside within all living beings, just as you reside in me. Your divine form is my real form . My Real form is "Shuddhatma." (Pure Atma).

Oh Shuddhatma Bhagwan ! With infinite devotion and oneness, I offer my salutations to you. I confess unto you, all mistakes * that I have committed in my ignorant state. I sincerely repent for these mistakes and ask for your pardon. Oh Lord ! Please forgive me, forgive me, forgive me and give me the strength not to repeat these mistakes again.

Oh Shuddhatma Bhagwan ! Please bless us all with such grace that this separation from you disappears and we attain oneness with you. May we remain One with you at all times.

(* Recall the past mistakes that you have committed)

Pratikraman : Process of Divine Apology

With Dada Bhagwan as my witness, I offer my salutations to the Pure Soul who is totally separate from the mind, speech and body of * _____

I recall my mistakes (aalochana) **

I apologize for these mistakes (pratikraman)

I affirm not to repeat these mistakes again (Pratyakhyaan)

Dearest Dada Bhagwan ! Grant me the strength to act in accordance with this firm resolution.

* name of the person hurt by you.

** recall the mistakes you committed with this person.

What Is the Gnan Vidhi?

It is a scientific spiritual process of gracing people with the experience of Self-realization. It is the gracing of real Knowledge that separates the Self from the non-Self or the worldly self. This session is different from the regular *satsangs* in the form of questions-answers sessions.

The Knowledge that manifested within Pujya Dadashri, also known as Dada Bhagwan in 1958, is the very same Knowledge that is graced upon all seekers through the medium of *Atmagnani* Param Pujya Deepakbhai, with the grace of Dada Bhagwan and the blessings of Pujya Niruma.

Why Should You Take Gnan – Knowledge of the Self?

1. To awaken and experience the Soul; your real Self.

2. Inner peace due to destruction of all wrong beliefs and the attainment of the right belief of 'I, the real Self am pure Soul'.

3. To attain liberation from the cycle of birth and death.

4. Demerit *karma* of infinite past lives are destroyed.

5. To experience eternal peace, happiness and harmony with all living beings.

6. To get solutions to carry out your worldly life through right understanding.

7. You finish paying off all past *karma* and you do not bind any new ones.

Is It Necessary for One to be Physically Present for the Gnan Vidhi?

1. *Gnan Vidhi* is the result of the *Gnani's* grace and blessings. It is necessary to attend this *Gnan Vidhi* in the direct presence of an *Atmagnani*.

2. Spiritual information acquired through watching *satsang* programs of Pujya Niruma and Pujya Deepakbhai on TV or VCD, books etc. can help you prepare the background for attaining *Gnan* but they cannot give you Self-realization.

3. Any instrument used for attaining *Gnan* can help you to attain peace but for awakening of the Soul, only the *Gnan* taken in the direct presence of an *Atmagnani* will give you the experience. For example if you want to light your candle, you need a real burning candle, a picture of a burning candle will not do.

- **You do not have to change your religion or your guru to attain this *Gnan*.**

- **You do not have to pay anything to attain this *Gnan*.**

Jai Sat Chit Anand

306.81 Bhagwan
Bhagwan, Dada,
Harmony in marriage
30519010065897

Books of Akram Vignan of Dada Bhagwan

1. Adjust Everywhere
2. Ahimsa : Non-Violence
3. Anger
4. Aptavani - 1
5. Aptavani - 2
6. Aptavani - 4
7. Aptavani - 5
8. Aptavani - 6
9. Aptavani - 8
10. Aptavani - 9
11. Autobiography of Gnani Purush A.M.Patel
12. Avoid Clashes
13. Brahmacharya : Celibacy Attained With Understanding
14. Death : Before, During & After...
15. Flawless Vision
16. Generation Gap
17. Harmony In Marriage
18. Life Without Conflict
19. Money
20. Noble Use of Money
21. Pratikraman : The master key that resolves all conflicts (Abridge & Big Volume)
22. Pure Love
23. Right Understanding to Help Others
24. Science of Karma
25. Science of Speech
26. Shree Simandhar Swami : The Living God
27. The Essence Of All Religion
28. The Fault Is Of the Sufferer
29. The Guru and The Disciple
30. Tri Mantra : The mantra that removes all worldly obstacles
31. Whatever Happened is Justice
32. Who Am I ?
33. Worries

'Dadavani' Magazine is published Every month

Persons to Contact

Dada Bhagwan Parivar

Adalaj : **Trimandir**, Simandhar City,
Ahmedabad-Kalol Highway, Adalaj,
Dist.: Gandhinagar - 382421, Gujarat, India.
Tel : (079) 39830100, **Email** : info@dadabhagwan.org

Ahmedabad : **Dada Darshan**, 5, Mamtapark Society,
Behind Navgujarat College, Usmanpura,
Ahmedabad- 380 014. **Tel.** : (079) 27540408

Rajkot : **Trimandir**, Ahmedabad-Rajkot Highway, Nr. Targhadiya
Cross Road, Maliyasan Village, Rajkot. **Cell.**: 9274111393

Bhuj : **Trimandir**, Behind Hill Garden, Airport Road,
Near Sahyognagar, Bhuj (Kutch). **Tel.** : (02832) 290123

Godhra : **Trimandir**, Village-Bhamaiya, Opp. FCI Godown, Godhra,
Dist.-Panchmahal. **Tel.** : (02672) 262300

Morbi : **Trimandir**, Village-Jepur, Morbi-Navlakhi Road, Morbi,
Dist.-Rajkot. **Tel.** : (02822) 297097

Vadodara : **Dada Mandir**, 17, Mama ni Pol (Street),
Opp. Raopura Police Station, Salatvada, Vadodara.
Cell. : 9924343335

Mumbai : Dada Bhagwan Parivar, **Cell.** : 9323528901

Bangalore : Dada Bhagwan Parivar, **Cell.** : 9590979099

U.S.A. : **Dada Bhagwan Vignan Institute** :
100, SW Redbud Lane, Topeka, Kansas 66606
Tel. : +1 877-505-DADA (3232) ,
Email : info@us.dadabhagwan.org

U.K.: **Dada Darshan (UK)**, Unit 2, Columbus House,
Stonefield Way, Ruislip, HA4 0JA
Tel. :+44 330-111-DADA (3232),
Email : info@uk.dadabhagwan.org

Kenya : +254 722 722 063   **Singapore** : +65 81129229

Australia : +61 421127947   **New Zealand** : +64 21 0376434

UAE : +971 557316937   **Germany** : +49 700 32327474

www.dadabhagwan.org, www.dadashri.org

Books of Akram Vignan of Dada Bhagwan

1. Adjust Everywhere
2. Ahimsa : Non-Violence
3. Anger
4. Aptavani 1
5. Aptavani 2
6. Aptavani 4
7. Aptavani 5
8. Aptavani 6
9. Aptavani 9
10. Autobiography of Gnani Purush A.M.Patel
11. Avoid Clashes
12. Brahmacharya : Celibacy Attained With Understanding
13. Death : Before, During & After...
14. Flawless Vision
15. Generation Gap
16. Harmony In Marriage
17. Life Without Conflict
18. Money
19. Noble Use of Money
20. Pratikraman : The master key that resolves all conflicts (Abridge & Big Volume)
21. Pure Love
22. Right Understanding to Help Others
23. Science of Karma
24. Science of Speech
25. Shree Simandhar Swami : The Living God
26. The Essence Of All Religion
27. The Fault Is Of the Sufferer
28. The Guru and The Disciple
29. Tri Mantra : The mantra that removes all worldly obstacles
30. Whatever Happened is Justice
31. Who Am I ?
32. Worries

'Dadavani' Magazine Is Published Every Month

Contacts

Dada Bhagwan Parivar

Adalaj : **Trimandir**, Simandhar City,
Main centre Ahmedabad-Kalol Highway, Adalaj,
Dist.: Gandhinagar - 382421, Gujarat, India.
Tel : +91 79 39830100, **Email :** info@dadabhagwan.org

Toll free inquiry number for USA & Canada
1-877-505-DADA (3232)

USA Email : info@us.dadabhagwan.org
Canada Email : info@ca.dadabhagwan.org

Ext.	Name of Activity/Center	Ext.	Name of Center
10	Gurupurnima Information	1019	Milwaukee Center
11	Satsang and Gnanvidhi	1007	Minneapolis Center
12	Books VCD and DVD	1025	Montreal Center
13	Dadavani Coordinators	1020	New Jersey Center
14	Kids Team	1021	New York Center
1011	Atlanta Center	1024	North California Center
1004	Birmingham Center	1022	Oregon Center
1012	Champaign Center	1002	Philadelphia Center
1027	Charlotte Center	1008	Phoenix Center
1005	Chicago Center	1003	Raleigh Center
1026	Dallas Center	1017	Simi Valley Center
1013	Houston Center	1015	Tampa Center
1009	Los Angeles Center	1006	Toronto Center
1016	Lowell Center	1010	Virginia Center
1018	Maryland Center	1023	Wilmington Center

Australia	: +61 421127947	**Singapore :**	+65 81129229
Germany	: +49 700 32327474	**Spain**	: +34 9221 33282
Kenya	: +254 722 722 063	**UAE**	: +971 557316937
New Zealand :	+64 21 0376434	**UK**	: +44 330-111-DADA (3232)
Brazil	: +55 11973372647		

Website : www.dadabhagwan.org